Everything About AI
in
100 Pages

Written
By
Edmond King

Table of Contents

CHAPTER 1: INTRODUCTION TO AI

1.1 What is Artificial Intelligence?

Definition of AI:

Artificial Intelligence (AI) refers to the creation of machines or software capable of performing tasks that typically require human intelligence. These tasks include understanding language, recognizing patterns, solving problems, making decisions, and learning from experience. Essentially, AI is the field of computer science focused on developing systems that can think, reason, and adapt autonomously.

AI encompasses a wide range of technologies, but at its core, it's about creating machines that can perform cognitive functions. The term "artificial" in AI highlights that the intelligence demonstrated by these machines is not natural, like that of humans, but is instead designed and engineered to mimic human behavior.

Everyday Examples of AI:

1. **Virtual Assistants**:
   Virtual assistants like Apple's **Siri**, Amazon's **Alexa**, and Google Assistant are some of the most common examples of AI. These assistants use speech recognition and natural language processing (NLP) to understand user commands and provide answers, play music, set reminders, or control smart home devices.

2. **Recommendation Systems**:
   Streaming platforms like **Netflix** and **Spotify** use AI to recommend movies, shows, or music based on your previous behavior. The system learns from your choices and refines its suggestions to make them more relevant over time.

3. **Autonomous Vehicles**:
   Self-driving cars, such as those developed by **Tesla** and **Waymo**, are powered by AI. These vehicles use AI systems to process data from sensors, cameras, and radar to navigate the road, avoid obstacles, and make decisions in real time.

4. **Fraud Detection**:
   Banks and **credit card companies** use AI algorithms to detect unusual behavior, such as fraudulent transactions. AI models analyze patterns in financial transactions to flag potential fraud before it happens.

AI vs. Human Intelligence:

While AI can replicate certain cognitive tasks, it differs significantly from human intelligence in several ways:

- **Speed and Scale**: AI can process vast amounts of data far faster than a human can. For example, AI can analyze millions of data points in seconds to detect patterns, something that would take humans years to do manually.

- **Specific Tasks**: AI is typically designed for specific tasks (this is often referred to as "narrow AI"), like playing chess or recognizing faces. In contrast, humans possess **general intelligence**, the ability to perform a wide variety of tasks.

- **Learning Capabilities**: AI learns from data and experience, but its learning process is structured and constrained. Humans can learn new skills more flexibly and apply knowledge across multiple domains.

Core Functions of AI:

To better understand AI, it's essential to break down its core functions, which represent the broad capabilities that make a system "intelligent."

1. **Perception**:
   AI can analyze data from the world through various sensory inputs, such as vision (e.g., facial recognition), hearing (e.g., speech recognition), and touch (e.g., robotics). Perception allows AI to recognize objects, understand speech, and navigate the environment.

2. **Reasoning**:
   AI systems make decisions and solve problems by using logical reasoning. For example, AI can analyze patterns, evaluate possible outcomes, and select the most optimal solution. This process involves algorithms and decision-making models that can mimic human reasoning.

3. **Learning**:
   Machine learning is a key aspect of AI. Through learning, AI systems improve over time by analyzing data. This learning process can be supervised (where the system is given labeled data), unsupervised (where the system finds patterns in unstructured data), or reinforcement-based (where the system learns from trial and error).

4. **Natural Language Processing (NLP)**:
   AI's ability to understand and generate human language is referred to as Natural Language Processing (NLP). This function allows machines to read, interpret, and respond to text or speech, enabling applications like chatbots, automated customer service, and language translation tools.

1.2 A Brief History of AI
Early Beginnings of AI:

The concept of AI was first proposed in the mid-20th century, and its development is deeply rooted in the works of several brilliant minds. While the idea of creating machines that think like humans had been pondered for centuries, it wasn't until the 1940s and 1950s that AI began to take shape as a formal scientific discipline.

Alan Turing:

Alan Turing, a British mathematician and computer scientist, is often regarded as the father of AI. In 1950, he published a paper titled "Computing Machinery and Intelligence," where he posed the question, "Can machines think?" Turing introduced the **Turing Test**, a benchmark for determining whether a machine could exhibit behavior indistinguishable from human intelligence. While the Turing Test isn't without its criticisms, it became an essential philosophical and theoretical foundation for the field of AI.

Turing's work laid the groundwork for the idea that machines could process information in ways similar to the human mind. He also developed the concept of the **Turing Machine**, an abstract model for computation, which became a cornerstone for computer science and AI development.

The Dartmouth Conference (1956):

The field of AI was officially born during the **Dartmouth Summer Research Project on Artificial Intelligence** in 1956. Led by computer scientist **John McCarthy**, the conference brought together prominent researchers to explore the possibility of creating machines that could simulate human intelligence. This event is often considered the official founding of AI as a field of study.

It was here that McCarthy, **Marvin Minsky**, **Nathaniel Rochester**, and **Claude Shannon** coined the term "Artificial Intelligence." The Dartmouth conference also set ambitious goals: that within a generation, machines would be able to perform any intellectual task that a human could. Although this vision was far too ambitious for the time, the conference helped launch AI research into the public and academic consciousness.

Early AI Systems:
Following the Dartmouth Conference, early AI systems were developed, though they were far simpler than today's AI applications. One of the first notable projects was **ELIZA**, created by **Joseph Weizenbaum** in 1964. ELIZA was a computer program designed to simulate a conversation with a therapist. The program used a rule-based system to "understand" and respond to typed inputs, and though rudimentary, it demonstrated the potential for machines to engage in human-like dialogue.

Another early AI system was the **General Problem Solver (GPS)**, developed by **Allen Newell** and **Herbert A. Simon**. GPS was designed to simulate human problem-solving by using a set of general rules and heuristics to solve a wide range of problems. However, despite its groundbreaking design, the system faced limitations due to the complexity of real-world problems.

The AI Winter:
AI experienced periods of great excitement and expectations, but it also faced significant setbacks. These setbacks are referred to as the **AI Winters**, times when funding and interest in AI research dwindled due to unmet expectations.

The first AI Winter occurred in the **1970s** after early AI systems proved to be much more limited than initially anticipated. AI researchers had overpromised on the capabilities of machines, and the field struggled to make meaningful progress. Systems that were once thought to be the future of AI—such as rule-based expert systems—faced challenges in dealing with the complexity and ambiguity of real-world data.

The second AI Winter came in the **1980s**, triggered by a collapse in the market for **expert systems**. These systems were designed to simulate human expertise in specific domains (like medical diagnosis), but they required vast amounts of manual input and were difficult to scale. Once again, the limitations of early AI were exposed, and many investors and research organizations pulled back.

The Resurgence of AI (Late 20th Century to Present):

AI faced a major resurgence in the 1990s and early 2000s, driven by several factors:

1. **Advancements in Computing Power:**
   The exponential increase in computational power, driven by Moore's Law (the observation that the number of transistors on a microchip doubles roughly every two years), made it possible to process large amounts of data much faster than before.

2. **Big Data:**
   The explosion of data from sources like social media, the internet, and sensors has provided AI systems with vast amounts of information to learn from. The availability of large datasets became a key enabler of machine learning algorithms.

3. **Machine Learning and Deep Learning:**
   Machine learning—a subset of AI that focuses on building algorithms that allow computers to learn from and make predictions based on data—became a major driving force in AI's resurgence. Early machine learning techniques like **support vector machines** and **decision trees** laid the groundwork for more advanced models. However, it was **deep learning**, a subfield of machine learning that uses multi-layered neural networks to model complex patterns in data, that truly propelled AI into the mainstream.

In the 2010s, breakthroughs in deep learning and neural networks led to significant advancements in speech recognition, image classification, natural language processing, and even AI-powered art and music generation.

Notable Milestones in Modern AI:

- **IBM's Deep Blue**: In 1997, Deep Blue, a chess-playing computer, defeated world champion **Garry Kasparov**, demonstrating the power of AI in strategic decision-making.

- **Google's AlphaGo**: In 2016, AlphaGo, developed by **DeepMind**, defeated world champion **Lee Sedol** at the game of Go, a feat that was once considered beyond the capabilities of AI.

- **Self-Driving Cars**: Companies like **Tesla** and **Waymo** are at the forefront of developing autonomous vehicles that use AI to navigate the world, making decisions based on sensor data in real time.

AI's resurgence has revolutionized many industries, including healthcare, finance, manufacturing, and entertainment, proving that much of the early hype surrounding AI was warranted—though not without significant trial and error along the way.

1.3 The Importance of AI in Today's World

AI's Ubiquity in Everyday Life:

Artificial Intelligence is no longer a futuristic concept; it has already become an integral part of our everyday lives. From voice assistants to personalized recommendations, AI is transforming how we interact with technology. We rely on AI systems in countless ways, often without even realizing it.

1. **Smart Devices and Virtual Assistants:** AI-driven virtual assistants like **Amazon's Alexa**, **Google Assistant**, and **Apple's Siri** have become household staples. These assistants use natural language processing (NLP) to

understand voice commands and perform tasks such as setting alarms, controlling smart home devices, and answering questions. They learn from user interactions and improve over time, making them more efficient and accurate in predicting user needs.

2. **Search Engines and Recommendations:** When you search for something on **Google**, AI is behind the scenes, sorting through vast amounts of data to provide the most relevant results. Similarly, **YouTube**, **Netflix**, and **Spotify** use AI to analyze your preferences and suggest content that matches your tastes, making your experience more personalized and enjoyable.

3. **Social Media:** AI plays a central role in social media platforms like **Facebook**, **Twitter**, and **Instagram**. These platforms use machine learning algorithms to analyze your behavior and recommend content—whether it's posts, ads, or people to follow. AI also powers facial recognition technology in photo tagging, helping users quickly organize and identify images.

4. **E-commerce and Retail:** When you shop online at platforms like **Amazon** or **eBay**, AI is at work analyzing your browsing and purchasing behavior. AI algorithms suggest products you might like based on your past purchases, search history, and even the behavior of other users with similar tastes. AI also helps optimize supply chains, manage inventory, and personalize marketing efforts, all of which improve the customer shopping experience.

The Impact of AI Across Industries:

AI is transforming entire industries by driving innovation, enhancing productivity, and solving complex problems. Here's how AI is making waves in various sectors:

1. **Healthcare:** AI is revolutionizing healthcare in ways

that were once unimaginable. It is enabling **faster and more accurate diagnoses** by analyzing medical images (such as X-rays and MRIs) with incredible precision. AI algorithms can detect early signs of diseases like cancer, helping doctors provide timely treatment.

- **Personalized Medicine**: AI analyzes patient data to develop personalized treatment plans. For instance, AI can predict how a patient might respond to different drugs, leading to more effective treatments with fewer side effects.

- **Drug Discovery**: AI is accelerating the process of discovering new drugs by analyzing vast datasets to identify potential compounds. In 2020, AI-driven drug discovery was instrumental in developing **COVID-19 vaccines** in record time.

2. **Finance:** The financial sector has been transformed by AI, with applications ranging from algorithmic trading to fraud detection. AI-powered systems can process vast amounts of data in real-time, identifying market trends and making split-second investment decisions.

- **Fraud Detection**: Banks use AI to detect fraudulent transactions by analyzing spending patterns and identifying anomalies. These systems are more effective than traditional methods, helping banks prevent fraud before it occurs.

- **Customer Service**: AI-powered chatbots and virtual assistants handle routine banking queries, improving customer service efficiency and reducing wait times.

3. **Retail and E-Commerce:** AI is enhancing the online shopping experience by predicting customer preferences and optimizing product recommendations.

By analyzing browsing behavior, purchase history, and even the behavior of other shoppers, AI ensures that customers receive highly personalized recommendations.

- **Supply Chain Management**: AI also plays a crucial role in managing supply chains. Algorithms forecast demand, optimize inventory, and streamline shipping routes to improve efficiency and reduce costs. During high-demand seasons like the holidays, AI helps retailers ensure they have the right products in stock and can deliver them quickly.

- **Customer Sentiment Analysis**: Retailers use AI to analyze customer reviews, social media posts, and feedback, helping them understand customer sentiment and adjust products, marketing strategies, and customer service.

4. **Transportation:** AI is shaping the future of transportation, with autonomous vehicles being one of the most high-profile applications. Self-driving cars, trucks, and drones are expected to revolutionize how goods and people move around the world.

- **Autonomous Vehicles**: Companies like **Tesla** and **Waymo** are leading the way in developing autonomous vehicles that use AI to process data from cameras, sensors, and radar to navigate roads, detect obstacles, and make decisions in real-time. The goal is to make transportation safer, more efficient, and less reliant on human drivers.

- **Traffic Management**: AI-powered traffic management systems use real-time data to optimize traffic flow, reduce congestion, and improve road safety. These systems analyze traffic patterns and adjust traffic signals, helping cities become smarter and more efficient.

AI and Global Challenges:

AI is not just reshaping industries; it also holds the potential to address some of the world's most pressing challenges. With the power of machine learning, data analytics, and predictive modeling, AI is being used to solve problems in areas such as climate change, healthcare, and education.

1. **Climate Change:** AI is helping combat climate change by predicting environmental trends, optimizing energy use, and improving sustainability practices. AI models can forecast weather patterns and help governments and organizations plan for natural disasters such as floods, hurricanes, and wildfires.

   - **Sustainable Energy**: AI-powered smart grids optimize the use of renewable energy sources, such as solar and wind, by balancing supply and demand. AI is also used to improve energy efficiency in buildings and manufacturing processes.

2. **Health Pandemics:** AI models were instrumental in predicting the spread of **COVID-19**, analyzing infection rates, and helping design intervention strategies. AI-powered systems are now being used to track and predict outbreaks, as well as develop vaccines and treatments more efficiently.

3. **Education:** AI is transforming education by personalizing learning experiences for students. AI-driven educational tools can adapt to individual learning styles and provide tailored content that helps students understand complex topics more easily.

   - **Tutoring Systems**: Virtual tutoring systems powered by AI help students with personalized feedback and guidance. These systems can track student progress, identify areas for improvement, and recommend resources to help them succeed.

1.4 Key Concepts in AI

To understand how AI systems work, it's essential to grasp several foundational concepts that underpin the field. These concepts are key to unlocking the potential of AI, and they span from basic algorithms to advanced machine learning techniques.

1.4.1 Machine Learning (ML)

Machine learning is a core subset of AI that focuses on enabling machines to learn from data and improve over time without being explicitly programmed. The key idea is to use algorithms that can identify patterns in data, make predictions, and adapt based on new information.

- **Supervised Learning**:
  In supervised learning, an AI system is trained on a labeled dataset, meaning the data comes with correct answers (labels). The goal is for the machine to learn a function that maps inputs to outputs, enabling it to predict the labels of new, unseen data. Common applications include image recognition, email filtering, and speech-to-text conversion.
  - **Example**: If a system is being trained to recognize pictures of cats and dogs, the dataset would include images labeled "cat" or "dog." The AI model learns to classify new images based on these labels.
- **Unsupervised Learning**:
  In unsupervised learning, the machine is provided with data that has no labels. The system must

find patterns and groupings in the data on its own. Techniques like **clustering** and **dimensionality reduction** are commonly used in unsupervised learning. These techniques help reveal hidden structures within data, such as customer segments or data points that are anomalies.

- **Example**: In customer segmentation, an unsupervised learning algorithm can group customers based on purchasing behavior without prior knowledge of the specific segments.

- **Reinforcement Learning**:
Reinforcement learning is a type of learning where an agent interacts with an environment, taking actions to maximize a reward. It learns by trial and error, receiving feedback (positive or negative) based on the consequences of its actions. This type of learning is particularly useful in robotics and gaming.

  - **Example**: In training a self-driving car, reinforcement learning allows the car to make decisions (e.g., turning or braking) based on feedback from its environment, such as avoiding obstacles or reaching a destination.

1.4.2 Deep Learning

Deep learning is a subset of machine learning that focuses on neural networks with many layers—hence the term "deep." These multi-layered neural networks are capable of automatically learning features from data without needing explicit feature engineering. Deep learning has enabled significant breakthroughs in fields like image recognition, natural language processing, and autonomous driving.

- **Neural Networks**:
Neural networks are computational models inspired

by the human brain. They consist of layers of interconnected nodes (also called neurons) that process information in a hierarchical way. The input layer receives the data, while the output layer produces predictions. The hidden layers in between transform the data at different levels of abstraction.

- **Example**: A deep learning model can identify objects in images by progressively learning from low-level features (like edges) to high-level features (like faces or cars).

- **Convolutional Neural Networks (CNNs)**: CNNs are a type of neural network particularly well-suited for image processing tasks. They use layers that apply filters to the input data, detecting patterns like edges, textures, and shapes. This makes them highly effective for image classification, facial recognition, and even medical image analysis.

  - **Example**: In healthcare, CNNs are used to analyze medical images (such as CT scans or X-rays) to detect anomalies, such as tumors.

- **Recurrent Neural Networks (RNNs)**: RNNs are designed to handle sequential data, making them ideal for tasks like speech recognition, language modeling, and time-series forecasting. Unlike traditional neural networks, RNNs have feedback loops that allow them to retain information from previous inputs, which helps them understand the context in sequential data.

  - **Example**: In natural language processing, RNNs are used for language translation, where the model needs to consider the order of words and their meaning in a sentence.

1.4.3 Natural Language Processing (NLP)

Natural Language Processing is a field of AI that focuses on the interaction between computers and human language. NLP enables machines to read, understand, and generate text in a way that is both meaningful and useful.

- **Text Analysis**:
  NLP techniques can analyze text for sentiment, intent, and key entities. For example, sentiment analysis determines whether a piece of text expresses positive, negative, or neutral feelings. NLP is widely used in customer service, social media monitoring, and content recommendation systems.
  - **Example**: Companies use NLP-powered chatbots to interact with customers and respond to inquiries by analyzing the text of the conversation.
- **Machine Translation**:
  NLP enables automatic language translation, such as translating a document from English to Spanish. Early translation systems struggled with accuracy, but deep learning and modern NLP techniques have significantly improved machine translation systems like **Google Translate**.
- **Speech Recognition and Generation**:
  NLP also powers speech recognition systems, enabling voice-based interfaces like virtual assistants and transcription software. Additionally, NLP helps generate natural-sounding responses (like in text-to-speech systems), making human-computer interaction more intuitive.

1.4.4 Computer Vision

Computer vision is the field of AI that focuses on enabling machines to interpret and understand visual data from the world, such as images and videos. This involves tasks such as image classification, object detection, and facial recognition.

- **Image Classification:**
  This task involves categorizing an image into predefined labels. For example, an AI system might classify images of animals into categories such as dogs, cats, and birds.

- **Object Detection:**
  Unlike image classification, object detection not only identifies objects in an image but also locates them within the image. For example, a computer vision system might be able to identify all the cars in a parking lot and mark their positions with bounding boxes.

- **Facial Recognition:**
  Facial recognition technology uses computer vision to identify or verify a person based on their facial features. It's widely used in security systems, such as unlocking phones or tracking people in crowds.

CHAPTER 2: MACHINE LEARNING AND ITS APPLICATIONS

2.1 Introduction to Machine Learning

Machine learning (ML) is one of the most significant advancements in AI, allowing systems to automatically learn from data and improve their performance without human intervention. It is the driving force behind many of today's AI systems, from recommendation engines to self-driving cars.

In simple terms, machine learning enables machines to recognize patterns and make predictions based on data. Instead of being explicitly programmed with a set of instructions, machine learning algorithms identify patterns and relationships in data, which allow them to make decisions or predictions when given new data.

Key Types of Machine Learning:

1. **Supervised Learning**:
   Supervised learning is the most commonly used form of machine learning. In this approach, a model is trained using a labeled dataset, which means the data includes both input features and corresponding output labels. The model learns to map the input data to the correct output and can then make predictions on new, unseen data.

   - **Examples**: Image classification, spam email detection, sentiment analysis.

2. **Unsupervised Learning**:
   Unsupervised learning involves training a model on a dataset without labeled outcomes. The goal is to identify patterns or structure within the

data. Common unsupervised learning tasks include clustering (grouping similar data points together) and dimensionality reduction (reducing the number of variables to simplify the data while preserving its essential structure).

- **Examples**: Market segmentation, anomaly detection, recommendation systems.

3. **Reinforcement Learning**:
Reinforcement learning involves training an agent to make decisions by interacting with an environment. The agent receives rewards or penalties based on its actions, and over time, it learns to optimize its behavior to maximize the total reward. This type of learning is often used in robotics, gaming, and self-driving cars.

- **Examples**: Game-playing AI (e.g., AlphaGo), robotics, autonomous vehicles.

2.2 Applications of Machine Learning

Machine learning is not just a theoretical concept; it has countless practical applications that have already begun transforming various industries. Below are some of the most impactful ways machine learning is being applied today:

1. **Healthcare**:
Machine learning is revolutionizing healthcare by improving diagnostics, personalized treatments, and drug discovery.

- **Medical Imaging**: ML algorithms analyze medical images such as X-rays, MRIs, and CT scans to identify patterns that may be invisible to the human eye. For example, deep learning models can detect early signs of conditions like cancer, often before symptoms appear.

- **Predictive Analytics**: ML models predict the

likelihood of patients developing certain conditions based on their medical history, lifestyle factors, and genetic data. This allows for early intervention and personalized care plans.

- **Drug Discovery**: ML is used to analyze large datasets of biological information, identifying potential drug candidates and predicting how they will interact with the body, thus speeding up the drug discovery process.

2. **Finance**:

The finance industry uses machine learning to detect fraud, assess risk, and optimize trading strategies.

- **Fraud Detection**: ML algorithms analyze transactions in real-time to identify unusual patterns that may indicate fraudulent activity. These systems can flag suspicious transactions, allowing banks to intervene before the fraud occurs.

- **Algorithmic Trading**: In trading, machine learning models are used to predict stock prices based on historical data and market trends. These algorithms can make split-second decisions on when to buy or sell assets, optimizing returns.

- **Credit Scoring**: ML is also used to assess creditworthiness by analyzing a borrower's financial history and other relevant data. This provides more accurate and fair credit scores than traditional methods.

3. **Retail and E-Commerce**:

Machine learning plays a crucial role in personalizing the customer experience and optimizing operations in the retail and e-commerce sectors.

- **Recommendation Systems**: One of the most visible applications of ML is in the form of recommendation engines. Websites like **Amazon** and **Netflix** use ML algorithms to suggest products or content based on a user's past behavior and the behavior of other similar users.

- **Demand Forecasting**: Retailers use ML models to predict demand for products, helping them optimize inventory levels and avoid stockouts. Accurate demand forecasting also reduces waste and improves supply chain efficiency.

- **Customer Segmentation**: Machine learning algorithms analyze customer data to segment them into groups based on purchasing behavior, preferences, and demographics. This allows businesses to target marketing campaigns more effectively.

4. **Transportation**:

The transportation industry is experiencing major disruptions due to machine learning, particularly in the development of autonomous vehicles and optimization of logistics.

- **Self-Driving Cars**: Companies like **Tesla** and **Waymo** are developing autonomous vehicles that rely heavily on ML to process sensor data (e.g., cameras, radar) and make real-time driving decisions. These vehicles are designed to safely navigate roads, avoid obstacles, and follow traffic rules.

- **Route Optimization**: ML is used in logistics

to optimize delivery routes, saving time and fuel. Algorithms analyze traffic patterns, road conditions, and delivery schedules to determine the most efficient routes for trucks and delivery drones.

- **Predictive Maintenance**: Machine learning can predict when vehicles or machinery are likely to fail, enabling companies to perform maintenance before breakdowns occur, thus minimizing downtime and repair costs.

5. **Marketing**:

Machine learning enables businesses to understand customer behavior and tailor their marketing strategies accordingly.

- **Targeted Advertising**: ML algorithms analyze user data to display highly targeted ads based on interests, browsing behavior, and demographic information. This results in more effective ad campaigns and higher conversion rates.

- **Customer Churn Prediction**: ML models analyze customer data to predict which users are most likely to cancel a service or stop purchasing. Companies can use this information to implement retention strategies and reduce churn.

- **Sentiment Analysis**: ML is used to analyze customer reviews, social media posts, and feedback to determine public sentiment toward a product or brand. This allows businesses to adjust their strategies and improve customer satisfaction.

6. **Entertainment and Media**:

Machine learning is transforming the entertainment industry, from content creation to content recommendation.

- **Content Recommendation**: Streaming platforms like **Netflix**, **Spotify**, and **YouTube** use machine learning to recommend personalized content based on user behavior, listening patterns, and preferences.
- **Content Creation**: ML is also being used in content generation, such as music composition, video editing, and even writing. Tools like **OpenAI's GPT-3** (which powers this conversation) are being used to create text and media automatically.

- **Audience Engagement**: ML algorithms help media companies predict which content will be popular with audiences, allowing them to produce shows, movies, and articles that resonate with their target demographics.

2.3 Applications of Deep Learning

Deep learning, a subset of machine learning, is responsible for many of the most impressive AI advancements in recent years. It leverages artificial neural networks with many layers (hence the term "deep") to automatically learn and extract complex patterns from large volumes of data. This approach has enabled breakthroughs in a variety of fields, from image and speech recognition to autonomous driving and natural language understanding.

2.3.1 Computer Vision

Computer vision is one of the most widely used applications of deep learning. By using convolutional neural networks (CNNs), deep learning models have achieved remarkable results in tasks that require the understanding and interpretation of images and videos.

- **Image Classification**:
  One of the earliest and most prominent applications of deep learning in computer vision is image classification, where the goal is to categorize an image into predefined classes. For example, deep learning models are used to classify objects, animals, and scenes in images. A model trained on a dataset of labeled images can learn to recognize and categorize new images with high accuracy.

  - **Example**: Deep learning models are used in security systems to identify faces and detect objects in surveillance footage.

- **Object Detection**:
  Beyond simply classifying images, deep learning algorithms can also locate and identify specific objects within an image. This is achieved by drawing bounding boxes around objects of interest, allowing for more detailed analysis. Object detection is used in a variety of applications, such as self-driving cars, where identifying pedestrians, vehicles, and road signs is crucial.

  - **Example**: Autonomous vehicles use deep learning for real-time object detection, allowing the vehicle to navigate and avoid obstacles.

- **Facial Recognition**:
  Deep learning has also revolutionized facial recognition systems. By learning to extract distinguishing features from a person's face, deep learning models can identify or verify individuals in photos and videos. These systems are now widely used for security, authentication, and personalized services.

  - **Example**: Smartphone manufacturers, such as

Apple with Face ID, use deep learning models to enable facial recognition for unlocking devices and making secure payments.

2.3.2 Natural Language Processing (NLP)

Deep learning has brought significant improvements to NLP, the field that enables machines to understand and generate human language. By using deep neural networks, machines can now perform tasks such as language translation, sentiment analysis, and question answering with near-human accuracy.

- **Language Translation**:
  Deep learning models, particularly those based on recurrent neural networks (RNNs) and more recently, transformer models, have dramatically improved the accuracy and fluency of machine translation. These models can translate text from one language to another by learning complex patterns in the structure of both languages.
    - **Example: Google Translate** uses deep learning to provide real-time translation for over 100 languages, helping break down language barriers globally.
- **Speech Recognition**:
  Speech recognition, which involves converting spoken language into text, has seen major advances due to deep learning. Models trained on large datasets of spoken language can accurately transcribe speech, even in noisy environments. This technology is now used in voice assistants, transcription services, and even healthcare for dictating medical notes.
    - **Example: Amazon's Alexa** and **Google Assistant** use deep learning models to understand and

process user commands spoken in natural language.

- **Text Generation**:
Deep learning models, such as **OpenAI's GPT-3**, have become highly skilled at generating coherent, contextually relevant text. These models can write articles, answer questions, and even engage in conversations, demonstrating the remarkable ability of deep learning to understand and produce human-like language.
  - **Example**: Chatbots and virtual assistants rely on deep learning to provide intelligent, context-aware responses to user queries.

2.3.3 Autonomous Systems

Deep learning is also a critical component in the development of autonomous systems, particularly in the fields of robotics and self-driving cars. By processing sensor data in real-time and learning from vast amounts of information, deep learning models enable machines to make decisions and take actions independently.

- **Autonomous Vehicles**:
Self-driving cars rely heavily on deep learning to interpret data from cameras, lidar, radar, and other sensors. These vehicles use deep learning to detect obstacles, understand traffic signs, and make driving decisions, allowing them to navigate roads safely and efficiently without human intervention.
  - **Example: Tesla's Autopilot** and **Waymo's self-driving cars** use deep learning to enable autonomous driving in various environments.
- **Robotics**:

Deep learning is used in robotics to help robots understand their environment, make decisions, and perform complex tasks. In industrial settings, robots use deep learning to sort objects, perform quality control checks, and even assemble products. In healthcare, robots with deep learning capabilities assist in surgery and patient care.

- **Example**: **Boston Dynamics' Spot robot** uses deep learning to navigate complex environments, such as construction sites and disaster zones.

2.3.4 Healthcare

Deep learning has immense potential in healthcare, particularly in areas such as diagnostics, treatment planning, and drug discovery. The ability of deep learning models to analyze large datasets and recognize intricate patterns has led to significant advancements in medical research and practice.

- **Medical Imaging**:
  Deep learning models are used to analyze medical images, such as MRIs, CT scans, and X-rays, to detect abnormalities like tumors, fractures, and diseases. These models can outperform traditional methods, offering faster and more accurate diagnoses.

  - **Example**: Deep learning models are used to detect early signs of **breast cancer** in mammograms, enabling earlier intervention and better outcomes.

- **Drug Discovery**:
  Deep learning models analyze vast amounts of data to predict how molecules interact and identify promising candidates for new drugs. This accelerates the drug discovery process and reduces the time required to bring new treatments to market.

> ○ **Example**: Companies like **Insilico Medicine** use deep learning to identify new drug candidates for diseases such as cancer and Alzheimer's.

2.3.5 Creativity and Content Generation

Deep learning is also making its mark in creative fields such as art, music, and literature. By learning from large datasets of creative works, deep learning models can generate new content that mimics human creativity.

- **Art Generation**:
  Deep learning models, particularly **generative adversarial networks (GANs)**, have been used to create stunning works of art that resemble those created by humans. These models learn to generate images by analyzing a collection of existing artworks and creating new pieces based on learned patterns.
  - ○ **Example**: AI-generated art has gained popularity, with platforms like **Artbreeder** allowing users to create unique digital artwork using deep learning.

- **Music Composition**:
  Deep learning models are also used to compose music. By training on a vast collection of music from various genres, these models can generate original compositions, often indistinguishable from works created by human musicians.
  - ○ **Example**: **OpenAI's MuseNet** can compose original music in various styles, from classical to contemporary genres, based on a given prompt.

CHAPTER 3: ETHICAL CONSIDERATIONS IN AI

3.1 The Importance of Ethics in AI

As artificial intelligence becomes increasingly integrated into our lives, it is crucial to examine the ethical implications of these technologies. While AI offers vast potential for improving efficiency, solving complex problems, and enhancing our quality of life, it also raises important ethical questions that must be addressed. These concerns include the impact of AI on jobs, privacy, bias, and decision-making.

AI systems are capable of influencing critical aspects of society, from healthcare and law enforcement to finance and education. As a result, ethical considerations are no longer optional but essential to ensuring that AI technologies are developed and deployed responsibly and equitably.

3.2 Bias in AI Systems

One of the most significant ethical concerns in AI is the potential for bias in AI models. Machine learning algorithms learn patterns from historical data, and if that data is biased, the resulting model can also exhibit bias. This can lead to unfair outcomes, especially in sensitive areas like hiring, criminal justice, healthcare, and lending.

- **Examples of Bias:**
  - **Hiring Algorithms:** If an AI system is trained on historical hiring data that reflects biased hiring practices (e.g., favoring one gender or ethnicity), the AI model may replicate these biases, resulting in discrimination against certain groups of candidates.

- **Predictive Policing**: AI systems used in predictive policing, which forecast where crimes are likely to occur or identify individuals at risk of committing crimes, can perpetuate racial or socioeconomic biases if trained on data that reflects historical prejudices in law enforcement.

- **Addressing Bias**:
  Researchers and developers are increasingly aware of the need to address bias in AI systems. Methods like diverse and representative training datasets, fairness algorithms, and bias audits are being implemented to ensure that AI systems are as unbiased and equitable as possible.

3.3 Privacy Concerns and Data Protection

AI systems rely heavily on data, and much of this data is personal and sensitive in nature. The use of personal data to train AI models raises significant privacy concerns, especially when individuals are unaware of how their data is being used or when that data is not adequately protected.

- **Data Collection and Consent**:
  Many AI systems require vast amounts of data to function effectively. This data may include sensitive personal information, such as health records, financial transactions, or online activity. Ethical concerns arise when data is collected without proper consent or when individuals are unaware of how their data is being used.

  - **Example**: Social media platforms and online services collect user data to train AI models, often without explicit consent. This can lead to concerns over how personal data is stored, shared, and used.

- **Data Security**:
Protecting the data used to train AI systems is paramount. If sensitive data is breached or exposed, it can lead to identity theft, financial loss, and other personal harms. The ethical responsibility lies in ensuring robust security measures to safeguard personal data from malicious actors.

  - **Example**: High-profile data breaches, such as those involving credit card companies or healthcare providers, demonstrate the risks associated with the mishandling of sensitive information.

3.4 Transparency and Accountability in AI Systems

As AI systems become more autonomous and decision-making processes become less transparent, it is essential to establish clear accountability structures. This includes understanding how AI systems make decisions and ensuring that there are mechanisms in place to hold those responsible for any harmful outcomes.

- **Explainability**:
AI models, especially complex deep learning systems, can be difficult to understand, even for experts. This lack of transparency, often referred to as the "black-box" problem, makes it challenging to explain how decisions are made by AI systems. For instance, in high-stakes areas like healthcare or criminal justice, it is crucial to know how an AI model arrived at its conclusions, especially when those decisions affect people's lives.

  - **Example**: If an AI system recommends a treatment

plan for a patient or predicts the likelihood of reoffending for a parolee, it is vital that the reasoning behind these decisions is transparent and understandable to doctors, judges, or other decision-makers.

- **Accountability**:
  When an AI system causes harm, it is crucial to determine who is responsible. Should the developer of the AI be held accountable for a biased or erroneous decision, or should responsibility lie with the organization that deployed the system? This question of accountability becomes particularly critical when AI systems are deployed in public or high-risk settings, such as policing, healthcare, and finance.

  - **Example**: If an autonomous vehicle causes an accident, determining whether the responsibility lies with the manufacturer, the software developer, or another party is an ethical and legal challenge.

3.5 The Impact of AI on Employment

The widespread adoption of AI is expected to have a significant impact on the job market. While AI can improve productivity and create new job opportunities, it can also lead to job displacement as machines and algorithms replace human labor in certain industries. This shift can exacerbate inequality and create economic challenges for workers who may not have the skills required for the new roles created by AI.

- **Job Displacement**:
  AI and automation are already being used to replace certain types of jobs, particularly in industries like manufacturing, retail, and transportation. For example, robots and AI-powered systems are being deployed in factories, warehouses, and even delivery services, reducing the need for human workers in these roles.

- **Example**: Self-checkout machines in grocery stores are reducing the need for cashiers, while autonomous trucks are expected to disrupt the trucking industry.

- **Job Creation**:
While some jobs may be displaced, AI also has the potential to create new roles in fields like AI development, data science, and machine learning. Additionally, AI can augment human workers, allowing them to focus on more complex tasks while AI handles repetitive or dangerous work.

  - **Example**: AI applications in healthcare, finance, and law are generating new opportunities for professionals with specialized skills in these areas.

3.6 The Role of Regulations in AI Ethics

As AI continues to advance, governments, regulatory bodies, and organizations are exploring ways to ensure that AI technologies are developed and used ethically. This includes creating frameworks to address issues such as bias, privacy, transparency, and accountability.

- **Global Standards**:
There is an increasing push for international standards and regulations that govern the use of AI. These regulations aim to create a global approach to ethical AI development, ensuring consistency and fairness across borders.

  - **Example**: The **European Union's General Data Protection Regulation (GDPR)** includes provisions that impact AI development, particularly in relation to data privacy and algorithmic transparency.

- **Ethical Guidelines**:
Many organizations are adopting ethical guidelines and principles for AI development. These include ensuring that AI systems are fair, transparent, and accountable, and that they prioritize human rights and well-being.
  - **Example**: The **Ethics Guidelines for Trustworthy AI**, developed by the EU, provides a framework for AI developers to ensure their systems are ethically sound.

CHAPTER 4: THE FUTURE OF AI

4.1 Emerging Trends in AI

As AI technologies evolve, new trends and breakthroughs are emerging that promise to significantly reshape the landscape of AI in the coming years. These trends span various subfields of AI, from machine learning and natural language processing to robotics and ethics.

- **Quantum Computing and AI**:
  One of the most exciting developments in the future of AI is the potential integration of quantum computing. Quantum computers, which use quantum bits (qubits) instead of classical bits, are expected to process information at speeds far beyond the capabilities of traditional computers. This could enable AI models to perform complex calculations and process vast datasets much more efficiently.

    - **Example**: Companies like **IBM** and **Google** are exploring the intersection of quantum computing and AI, aiming to accelerate problem-solving in areas like drug discovery, optimization, and material science.

- **AI in Edge Computing**:
  Edge computing refers to processing data closer to where it is generated, rather than relying solely on centralized cloud data centers. As IoT devices become more widespread, AI is being integrated into edge devices to perform real-time processing and decision-making without the need for constant cloud connectivity. This trend is expected to expand the use of AI in areas like autonomous vehicles, smart cities, and industrial automation.

- **Example**: AI-powered cameras, sensors, and drones that operate independently on the edge can make real-time decisions in applications like security surveillance and agriculture monitoring.

- **Explainable AI (XAI)**:
  While deep learning and other advanced AI models have made remarkable strides, the lack of transparency in how these models make decisions (the "black-box" problem) remains a significant challenge. Explainable AI (XAI) aims to create models that are not only accurate but also interpretable by humans, allowing for better understanding and trust in AI decisions. The future of AI will likely see more emphasis on developing systems that are explainable and accountable.

  - **Example**: Medical professionals may demand XAI systems that can explain the reasoning behind a diagnosis or treatment recommendation, enabling them to make informed decisions.

4.2 AI's Impact on the Workforce

The integration of AI into various industries is expected to dramatically alter the global workforce. While some jobs may be displaced due to automation, AI is also likely to create new opportunities and transform existing roles.

- **Job Displacement and Transformation**:
  As AI systems become more capable, there is concern about the automation of many routine and manual tasks, particularly in industries like manufacturing, retail, and transportation. For example, autonomous vehicles could replace truck drivers, while AI-powered chatbots may reduce the need for customer service representatives. However, many of these technologies also have the potential to augment human workers,

enabling them to focus on more creative or complex tasks.

- Example: The rise of AI-powered virtual assistants like **Siri** or **Google Assistant** may reduce the demand for call center workers but create opportunities in AI development, training, and system management.

- **New Job Opportunities**:
AI will likely create new jobs, especially in fields that require expertise in machine learning, data science, robotics, and AI ethics. As businesses and industries continue to adopt AI technologies, the demand for professionals skilled in these areas will increase. Furthermore, AI is expected to enhance the productivity of human workers, allowing them to perform tasks more efficiently and focus on high-value activities.

- Example: The growth of AI startups and established companies adopting AI technology will drive demand for data scientists, machine learning engineers, and AI ethicists.

4.3 AI in Healthcare: Revolutionizing Medicine

AI's potential in healthcare is vast and transformative. As technology advances, AI will play an increasingly important role in improving patient outcomes, optimizing healthcare systems, and even enabling new forms of personalized medicine.

- **AI-Powered Diagnostics**:
AI systems have already shown promise in diagnosing diseases from medical images, such as identifying tumors in radiology scans or detecting diabetic retinopathy in eye exams. As AI continues to improve, it could be used to analyze genetic data, predict disease outbreaks, and monitor chronic conditions.

- **Example**: AI models like **DeepMind's AI** have been shown to outperform human radiologists in certain tasks, such as detecting eye diseases from retinal scans.

- **Personalized Medicine**:
AI can help create tailored treatment plans based on a patient's unique genetic makeup, lifestyle, and medical history. By analyzing large datasets of patient information, AI can identify patterns and suggest personalized therapies that are more likely to be effective for individual patients.

  - **Example**: AI-driven platforms are being developed to analyze genetic data to identify individuals who may be at higher risk for certain conditions, enabling earlier intervention and more targeted treatment.

- **Drug Discovery and Development**:
The traditional drug discovery process can be slow, expensive, and risky. AI, however, can accelerate this process by analyzing large datasets, predicting which compounds are most likely to work, and identifying potential side effects. This could lead to faster development of new drugs and therapies, potentially saving lives and reducing costs.

  - **Example**: AI models are being used to predict which molecules might be effective in treating diseases like cancer, significantly reducing the time and cost of research and development.

4.4 AI and Society: Balancing Progress and Risk

As AI continues to evolve, it is crucial to consider the broader societal implications. The rise of AI will undoubtedly bring about significant changes, but these changes must be managed carefully to ensure they benefit society as a whole.

- **Ethical AI Development:**
  The future of AI hinges on the ethical considerations made during its development. It is crucial that AI systems are designed to be transparent, accountable, and free from bias. Additionally, AI must be used in ways that benefit humanity and do not exacerbate existing inequalities. Governments, businesses, and researchers must work together to create ethical guidelines and regulations that ensure AI is developed responsibly.
  - **Example:** The **OECD AI Principles** outline recommendations for the responsible development and use of AI, focusing on ensuring that AI benefits people and respects fundamental rights.

- **AI for Social Good:**
  AI has the potential to address some of society's most pressing challenges, from climate change and public health to education and poverty alleviation. By applying AI to social good initiatives, it is possible to create positive societal impact and improve the quality of life for billions of people.
  - **Example:** AI-driven platforms are being used to predict and manage natural disasters, such as hurricanes and wildfires, by analyzing environmental data and providing early warnings.

4.5 Conclusion: A Future Shaped by AI

The future of AI holds immense promise, with advancements in technology set to revolutionize industries, improve lives, and address some of the world's most complex challenges. However, to ensure that AI's benefits are maximized and its risks minimized, it is essential that ethical considerations remain at the forefront of AI development.

As AI continues to evolve, it will reshape how we work, learn, communicate, and interact with the world around us. By balancing innovation with caution, we can unlock the full potential of AI while ensuring that it serves the common good and improves society as a whole.

CHAPTER 5: AI IN EVERYDAY LIFE

5.1 Introduction to AI in Daily Life

AI is no longer a technology confined to research labs or the industrial sector; it is firmly embedded in everyday life, with millions of people interacting with AI systems daily, often without even realizing it. AI has transformed how we interact with technology, making everyday tasks easier, more personalized, and more efficient. From enhancing our interactions with smartphones to automating home management, AI is shaping the way we live, work, and play.

As AI continues to mature, it will become even more integrated into our routines. The development of more advanced algorithms and more capable AI-driven devices is creating an ecosystem where technology becomes an extension of ourselves, anticipating our needs and optimizing our lives.

5.2 AI in Consumer Electronics

Consumer electronics are among the most visible areas where AI is making an impact. AI is used in everything from smartphones and TVs to smart appliances, and it has become a central feature of many devices that we interact with daily.

- **Smartphones and AI**:
  Smartphones are increasingly AI-powered, utilizing machine learning to enhance user experience. AI not only improves the hardware but also provides software-driven enhancements that make these devices more intuitive. Personal assistants like **Siri**, **Google Assistant**, and **Bixby** rely on voice recognition algorithms to provide users with information, set reminders, and even control other devices.

- **Example**: AI-powered **camera enhancements** in smartphones are making photography easier for users. AI helps optimize settings based on the scene (e.g., portrait, night mode) and even enhances pictures by removing noise and adjusting lighting.

- **Deep Dive**: AI systems in smartphones also use **natural language processing (NLP)** to better understand and predict user intentions. For example, NLP enables assistants to process commands like "Remind me to pick up groceries at 5 PM" with a high degree of accuracy, even if the language used is informal.

- **Smart Home Devices**:
Smart home devices powered by AI are rapidly becoming the center of modern homes. **Amazon Echo** and **Google Nest Hub** use AI to understand voice commands, control lights, thermostats, and other connected devices, and even play music or provide news updates.

  - **Example**: AI in smart thermostats, like the **Nest Learning Thermostat**, learns user preferences and automatically adjusts room temperature based on time of day, weather conditions, and whether or not someone is at home. This helps optimize energy use, leading to cost savings and environmental benefits.

  - **Deep Dive**: These devices are also learning how users interact with them. Over time, the AI system gains insights into their schedules, preferences, and routines. This adaptation allows the devices to act more like personal assistants, proactively adjusting the environment to user needs.

5.3 AI in Online Services and Social Media

AI is the backbone of many online platforms and services, transforming how we shop, connect, and consume content. Platforms like social media and e-commerce rely on AI to enhance user experiences, boost engagement, and drive revenue.

- **Social Media Algorithms**:
  Platforms like **Facebook**, **Instagram**, and **TikTok** are built around AI algorithms that determine what content appears in users' feeds. These algorithms continuously learn from user interactions to make better predictions about which posts, videos, and advertisements users will engage with. They use data from various sources, such as likes, shares, comments, and even the time spent viewing content.

  - **Example: Instagram's Explore page** uses AI to suggest posts from accounts users may not follow yet but might be interested in based on their engagement patterns and similar users' behavior.

  - **Deep Dive**: Social media platforms employ a form of AI called **reinforcement learning**, where algorithms are constantly adjusting their behavior based on feedback from users. For example, if you like posts related to fitness or cooking, the algorithm will increase the frequency of such posts appearing on your feed, continuously refining its recommendations.

- **E-commerce and AI**:
  The power of AI in e-commerce lies in personalization.

AI tracks customer behavior and uses this data to recommend products, predict future purchases, and optimize shopping experiences. **Amazon**, for example, has refined its recommendation engine to suggest products based on browsing history, past purchases, and even items viewed but not bought.

- **Example: Amazon's AI-powered recommendation system** is so sophisticated that it can predict what you might want to buy even before you search for it. This not only improves the user experience but also boosts sales for retailers by guiding customers toward items they are likely to purchase.
- **Deep Dive**: These recommendation systems are powered by **collaborative filtering**, where algorithms analyze the behavior of similar customers to predict what an individual user might be interested in. This has revolutionized the way online shopping works, significantly increasing conversion rates.

5.4 AI in Healthcare and Fitness

In healthcare, AI is helping doctors make better decisions and enabling individuals to monitor their health more proactively. AI applications in fitness are also providing personalized wellness guidance to individuals, improving their overall health and lifestyle.

- **AI-Powered Diagnostics**:
  One of the most exciting applications of AI in healthcare is in diagnostics. AI algorithms can analyze medical images to detect conditions like cancer, diabetic retinopathy, and more. These AI tools are often

used alongside human doctors to enhance diagnostic accuracy and speed.

- **Example**: **DeepMind's AI** can analyze retinal scans to detect early signs of eye disease, often identifying conditions faster and more accurately than human doctors.

- **Deep Dive**: AI tools like **IBM Watson** assist in diagnosing complex diseases by analyzing vast amounts of medical literature, clinical trial data, and patient records. This allows healthcare providers to get quicker, more accurate recommendations for diagnosis and treatment plans, reducing human error and improving patient outcomes.

- **Personalized Medicine**:
AI's ability to process large datasets also opens the door to personalized medicine, where treatments and medications are tailored to individual patients based on their genetic makeup and lifestyle. AI can help analyze genetic data to determine how different patients might respond to specific treatments, leading to more effective and targeted therapies.

  - **Example**: **Tempus** is a technology company that uses AI and machine learning to analyze clinical and molecular data to help doctors make personalized decisions for cancer patients.

- **Health Monitoring and Wearables**:
Devices like **Fitbit**, **Apple Watch**, and **Garmin** track users' health metrics, such as steps, heart rate, and sleep patterns. These devices rely on AI to provide insights and recommendations, empowering users to take control of their health.

  - **Example**: **Apple Watch's ECG** and **fall detection**

features provide users with real-time insights into their heart health and alert emergency services if a fall is detected, demonstrating AI's growing role in proactive health management.

5.5 AI in Entertainment and Media

The entertainment industry is undergoing significant changes due to AI, which is being used to generate content, create more immersive experiences, and optimize consumption patterns. Whether in film, music, or gaming, AI is enhancing creativity and improving the user experience.

- **AI in Content Creation**:
  AI tools are being used to create music, art, and even scripts. These systems can generate new pieces of art or music based on a set of instructions or training data, offering new avenues for creativity and collaboration.

    - **Example**: **Amper Music** is an AI tool that allows users to create music by selecting mood, genre, and instruments, enabling even non-musicians to generate professional-sounding tracks.

- **AI in Streaming Services**:
  Netflix, **Spotify**, and other streaming platforms have become AI-powered recommendation engines. These platforms analyze users' past behavior, including what they've watched or listened to, and suggest similar content.

    - **Example**: **Spotify's Discover Weekly** uses AI to curate playlists based on your listening habits and the listening patterns of users with similar preferences.

- **AI in Video Games**:
  AI in gaming is increasingly focused on enhancing

realism and adapting the gaming experience. AI is used for procedural content generation, such as creating random levels or quests in games like **Minecraft** or **No Man's Sky**.

- Example: AI in games like **FIFA** is used to create more realistic player behaviors and to adjust difficulty dynamically to match a player's skill level, ensuring a balanced and immersive experience.

5.6 AI in Transportation and Autonomous Vehicles

The transportation industry is one of the most visible sectors where AI is expected to have a profound impact. Autonomous vehicles are a prime example of AI at work, but AI is also optimizing public transit systems, improving traffic management, and enhancing safety.

- **Autonomous Vehicles:**
  Companies like **Tesla**, **Waymo**, and **Uber** are pioneering the development of self-driving cars, which rely on machine learning algorithms to interpret data from sensors, cameras, and radar to navigate roads, make decisions, and avoid obstacles.

  - Example: **Tesla's Autopilot** system uses deep learning to control the car's steering, speed, and braking while driving on highways. The system improves over time with updates based on real-world driving data.

- **AI in Traffic Management:**
  Cities are increasingly turning to AI to optimize traffic flow, reduce congestion, and improve road safety. AI can adjust traffic signals in real-time based on the flow of vehicles and pedestrians, improving traffic efficiency and reducing delays.

- **Example**: In **Barcelona**, AI-powered traffic lights and traffic management systems help reduce congestion by analyzing traffic patterns and adjusting light timings to smooth traffic flow.

5.7 Conclusion

As AI continues to evolve, it will play an increasingly central role in everyday life, shaping how we work, communicate, shop, entertain ourselves, and manage our health. The potential of AI to enhance convenience, personalization, and efficiency is immense, but it also brings challenges related to privacy, ethics, and employment. Navigating these challenges while maximizing the benefits of AI will be key to ensuring its positive impact on society.

5.8 AI in Financial Services

AI is transforming the financial sector by improving security, streamlining processes, and offering personalized services. AI is used in a wide variety of applications, from fraud detection to automated financial advising, and even in the development of new financial products.

- **AI in Banking**:
  Banks and financial institutions are using AI to offer more personalized services, optimize decision-making, and reduce operational costs. AI algorithms analyze vast amounts of data, identifying trends and providing insights that human analysts might miss.
  - **Example**: **HSBC** has implemented AI-powered fraud detection systems that analyze transaction patterns in real-time. If a transaction seems suspicious, the system can alert the bank and even block the transaction to prevent fraud.
  - **Deep Dive**: AI-driven **chatbots** are also used in banking, handling customer inquiries such

as checking balances, transferring funds, or explaining account features. These chatbots use natural language processing to understand and respond to user requests efficiently, improving customer satisfaction and reducing wait times.

- **AI in Credit Scoring**:
Traditional credit scoring models rely on a limited set of data, but AI systems can take into account a wider variety of factors, offering more accurate credit scores. By analyzing a range of financial behaviors, AI can assess a person's creditworthiness with greater precision, allowing for more inclusive lending.
  - **Example: Upstart**, a fintech company, uses machine learning algorithms to provide alternative credit scoring, helping individuals who may not have a traditional credit history access loans.
- **Algorithmic Trading**:
AI is also used in the world of stock markets and trading. AI-driven systems can analyze market conditions, financial reports, and social media sentiment in real-time to predict market movements and optimize trading strategies.

  - **Example: Robo-advisors** like **Betterment** and **Wealthfront** use AI to create personalized investment portfolios for individuals. These platforms use algorithms to rebalance portfolios based on market trends and the client's risk profile, providing automated investment services without human intervention.

5.9 AI in Education
AI is revolutionizing education by offering personalized learning

experiences, automating administrative tasks, and providing new ways for students and teachers to interact with content.

- **Personalized Learning**:
  AI-powered systems can analyze students' strengths and weaknesses, providing tailored learning materials to help them progress at their own pace. These systems adjust content difficulty and offer instant feedback, ensuring that no student is left behind.
  - **Example**: **Knewton**, an adaptive learning platform, uses AI to personalize lessons based on a student's performance. By continually adjusting the content and pace, it helps learners engage with the material more effectively.

- **AI Tutors and Assistants**:
  AI tutors can provide additional support outside of the classroom. These tutors can answer students' questions, help with homework, and even teach new concepts. This offers an on-demand learning experience that complements traditional classroom education.
  - **Example: Duolingo**, a popular language-learning app, uses AI to personalize language lessons based on a learner's progress, adjusting difficulty levels and introducing new words based on mastery.

- **Administrative Efficiency**:
  AI is helping educational institutions streamline administrative tasks such as grading, attendance tracking, and scheduling. By automating these processes, AI allows teachers to spend more time focusing on student interaction and instruction.
  - **Example**: AI-driven grading tools can automatically grade multiple-choice and essay-based assignments, saving teachers significant

time. This system also provides immediate feedback to students, allowing them to improve their performance in real-time.

5.10 AI in Retail and Customer Service

AI is transforming the retail industry by enhancing customer experiences, streamlining inventory management, and driving personalized marketing efforts. Retailers are leveraging AI to anticipate customer needs, reduce costs, and improve overall service quality.

- **Personalized Shopping Experiences**:
  Retailers use AI to provide customers with personalized recommendations, tailored promotions, and personalized shopping experiences. By analyzing past shopping behavior and demographic data, AI can predict what products a customer is most likely to purchase.
  - **Example**: **Amazon** uses AI to recommend products based on a user's browsing history and past purchases, creating a more personalized shopping experience and driving sales.

- **AI in Customer Support**:
  Many companies use AI-driven chatbots and virtual assistants to handle customer service requests. These bots can address common inquiries, guide users through troubleshooting steps, and even help with purchasing decisions.
  - **Example**: **Sephora's chatbot** helps customers find products based on preferences such as skin type, fragrance preferences, or makeup styles, providing personalized product suggestions and even virtual try-ons.

- **AI for Inventory Management**:

Retailers are using AI to manage inventory more efficiently. AI-powered systems predict demand trends, optimize stock levels, and automatically reorder products when inventory runs low.

- **Example: Walmart** uses AI to monitor inventory levels across its stores and supply chain, ensuring that products are always in stock and preventing overstocking, which leads to excess inventory costs.

5.11 AI in Transportation and Urban Planning

AI's influence on transportation goes beyond autonomous vehicles. It is also enhancing urban mobility, optimizing infrastructure, and providing better public transportation services. AI is being used in smart city planning, traffic management, and predicting transportation needs.

- **AI in Public Transportation**:
  AI-powered systems are improving the efficiency and reliability of public transit. AI can predict passenger demand, optimize bus and train schedules, and ensure that services are adjusted according to peak hours or special events. This reduces wait times and helps manage congestion.

  - **Example: Citymapper**, a navigation app, uses AI to analyze real-time data from multiple transportation systems to recommend the fastest and most efficient routes for users. This service combines data from buses, trains, and even bikes to offer multimodal travel solutions.

- **AI in Smart Cities**:
  Cities around the world are adopting AI to become "smarter" and more sustainable. AI is used to monitor air quality, manage energy consumption, and

optimize waste management. Additionally, AI-powered surveillance and data analytics are helping law enforcement agencies increase safety and prevent crime.

- ○ **Example**: **Barcelona** has implemented an AI-driven system to manage traffic flow. The system collects data from traffic sensors, cameras, and GPS to optimize traffic signals, improve safety, and reduce congestion. It also helps reduce fuel consumption by managing traffic more efficiently.

- **AI in Ride-Sharing and Mobility**:
  Ride-sharing services like **Uber** and **Lyft** are leveraging AI to optimize driver routes, predict passenger demand, and set prices dynamically. The algorithms used by these companies adjust prices based on real-time demand, ensuring that drivers are efficiently dispatched to meet passenger needs.

  - ○ **Example**: **Uber's AI-driven pricing model** uses dynamic pricing algorithms to adjust fare prices in real-time, factoring in demand, location, and time of day. This allows the company to manage rider demand and incentivize drivers to operate in high-demand areas.

5.12 AI in Security and Surveillance

AI is increasingly being used for security and surveillance purposes, both in the public and private sectors. Its ability to process vast amounts of data quickly and detect patterns makes it an invaluable tool for crime prevention, safety monitoring, and personal security.

- **AI in Surveillance Systems**:
  AI-driven surveillance cameras can recognize faces, detect suspicious behaviors, and analyze crowd

patterns. These systems are used by governments, law enforcement, and private companies to enhance security and protect assets.

- **Example: Facial recognition technology** is used by companies like **Amazon Rekognition** to scan crowds for potential security threats or identify individuals in large public spaces. This is increasingly being used for access control in airports, stadiums, and office buildings.

- **Deep Dive:** AI-enabled cameras can also detect anomalies such as unusual movement patterns, abandoned objects, or unauthorized access. These AI systems reduce the need for human operators to manually monitor feeds, allowing for faster response times.

- **AI in Cybersecurity:**

AI is also playing a critical role in the field of cybersecurity, where it is used to detect and respond to cyber threats in real-time. AI can analyze network traffic, identify vulnerabilities, and even prevent attacks before they happen by recognizing malicious activity.

- **Example: Darktrace**, an AI cybersecurity company, uses machine learning to detect and respond to potential threats in real-time by analyzing network behavior and identifying deviations from normal activity patterns.

- **Deep Dive:** These AI systems are constantly evolving as they learn from new data. The more they process, the better they become at detecting subtle signs of cyberattacks, helping prevent incidents like data breaches and ransomware attacks.

5.13 AI in Marketing and Advertising

AI has revolutionized the marketing and advertising industries by enabling hyper-targeted campaigns and personalized messaging. With the help of AI, companies can analyze consumer data, predict trends, and automate campaigns with a high degree of accuracy.

- **Targeted Advertising**:
  AI algorithms are used to analyze user behavior and predict which advertisements are most likely to resonate with a given individual. By using data from browsing history, search queries, and social media activity, AI can deliver more personalized and effective ads.
  - **Example**: **Google Ads** uses AI to serve personalized advertisements based on a user's search history, location, and interests. This increases the likelihood of conversion and improves ROI for advertisers.
  - **Deep Dive**: One common method used in targeted advertising is **programmatic advertising**, where AI is used to buy and place ads in real-time, adjusting bids and targeting based on user behavior and engagement levels.
- **AI in Content Creation and Curation**:
  AI is also being used to generate content and curate media. Tools like **ChatGPT** and **Jasper AI** are used to write articles, social media posts, and even advertisements. These AI systems analyze vast amounts of text to create content that is relevant and engaging for specific audiences.
  - **Example**: **The Washington Post** uses an AI system called **Heliograf** to generate news

articles, especially for topics like sports and finance, where data can be easily turned into stories.

- **Customer Insights**:
  AI is used to analyze customer sentiment, feedback, and social media interactions to gain insights into consumer preferences and improve products and services.

  - **Example**: Companies like **Salesforce** use AI-powered analytics tools to analyze customer data, identifying patterns and insights that help businesses create more targeted campaigns and enhance customer satisfaction.

5.14 The Future of AI in Everyday Life

The future of AI in daily life looks incredibly promising. As AI technologies continue to evolve, they will become even more embedded in our routines, potentially revolutionizing how we live in ways that are hard to predict. However, this widespread adoption of AI will also require addressing several challenges, including privacy concerns, job displacement, and ethical implications.

- **Ethical Considerations**:
  As AI becomes more integrated into everyday life, questions around data privacy, bias in algorithms, and the ethical use of AI are becoming increasingly important. Governments, organizations, and tech companies will need to work together to establish guidelines and regulations that ensure AI is used responsibly.

  - **Example**: The **EU's General Data Protection Regulation (GDPR)** includes provisions related to AI, such as the right for individuals to know when they are being profiled and the ability to opt-out of certain forms of automated decision-making.

. **Job Displacement**:
AI is expected to transform the workforce, automating many tasks traditionally performed by humans. While this could lead to increased productivity, it also raises concerns about job displacement and the future of work. Reskilling and upskilling will be essential to help workers adapt to the changing job market.

  ○ **Example**: The rise of **AI-powered chatbots** in customer service roles has already led to job displacement in some sectors. However, this also creates new opportunities in AI management, data analysis, and machine learning.

. **Personal Assistants and Future Technologies**:
In the future, personal AI assistants will become even more capable, potentially managing many aspects of daily life. These assistants will be able to anticipate our needs, communicate seamlessly across devices, and even handle complex tasks like managing finances or personal health.

  ○ **Example**: Future AI assistants could go beyond current capabilities like Siri and Alexa, learning and adapting to personal preferences in ways that feel almost human-like. For instance, AI might be able to schedule appointments, manage budgets, and even negotiate on behalf of the user.

5.15 Conclusion

AI has already begun to transform everyday life in profound ways, and as the technology continues to advance, it will likely become even more ingrained in how we live and interact with the world around us. While the promise of AI brings exciting possibilities, it also presents challenges that need to be addressed carefully. In the end, AI is not just a tool but an extension of human potential that has the power to enhance every aspect of our lives.

5.16 AI in Healthcare and Medicine

One of the most impactful areas of AI adoption is in healthcare. AI is transforming diagnostics, treatment planning, drug discovery, and patient care, making the healthcare system more efficient and personalized.

- **AI in Diagnostics**:
  AI-powered tools are revolutionizing how doctors diagnose diseases. Machine learning algorithms are used to analyze medical images, such as X-rays, MRIs, and CT scans, identifying patterns that may be too subtle for human doctors to detect. AI can also help in diagnosing rare diseases by cross-referencing a vast amount of medical data.
    - **Example: IBM Watson Health** has developed AI systems that analyze medical records and research to help doctors diagnose diseases like cancer. The AI's ability to process vast datasets allows it to suggest possible diagnoses that a human doctor might not immediately consider.

- **AI in Drug Discovery**:
  The process of drug discovery is long, expensive, and complex. AI is helping researchers find new drugs faster by predicting how different compounds will interact with biological targets. This speeds up the process of identifying promising drug candidates, potentially saving years of research and development time.
    - **Example: Atomwise**, an AI company, uses machine learning to predict which drug molecules will be effective in treating diseases. This approach has accelerated the discovery of treatments for diseases like Ebola and multiple sclerosis.

- **AI in Personalized Medicine**:
  AI is also paving the way for more personalized treatments. By analyzing data from genetic testing, medical records, and lifestyle factors, AI can help tailor medical treatments to individual patients. This reduces the trial-and-error approach often seen in healthcare, leading to better outcomes and fewer side effects.
  - **Example: Tempus**, a technology company, uses AI to analyze clinical and molecular data to help doctors make more informed treatment decisions for cancer patients. Their platform uses data from genetic sequencing to find the best treatments for individual patients.

- **AI in Robotic Surgery**:
  Robotics powered by AI is being used to assist in surgical procedures, allowing for greater precision, smaller incisions, and faster recovery times. AI is being integrated into robotic systems to improve surgical planning, reduce human error, and enhance the accuracy of procedures.
  - **Example**: The **da Vinci Surgical System** is a robotic platform that allows surgeons to perform minimally invasive surgery with greater precision. AI algorithms help guide the robot during surgery, providing real-time feedback to the surgeon.

- **AI in Virtual Health Assistants**:
  Virtual health assistants powered by AI are becoming increasingly popular for providing healthcare advice, tracking symptoms, and even managing chronic conditions. These assistants can offer 24/7 support, answering health-related questions, scheduling appointments, and providing medication reminders.

> ○ **Example:** **Babylon Health**, an AI-powered telemedicine platform, allows users to consult with a virtual doctor for diagnosis, prescriptions, and health advice. By leveraging AI, it offers affordable healthcare access, especially in underserved regions.

5.17 AI in Manufacturing and Industry

AI is also making a significant impact on the manufacturing sector, optimizing production processes, enhancing quality control, and reducing downtime.

- **Predictive Maintenance:**
  One of the key applications of AI in manufacturing is predictive maintenance. By analyzing data from equipment sensors and historical maintenance records, AI can predict when a machine is likely to fail, allowing companies to perform maintenance before a breakdown occurs. This reduces downtime and increases the longevity of equipment.
  - ○ **Example: General Electric (GE)** uses AI-powered predictive maintenance systems in their turbines and jet engines. These systems monitor the equipment's performance in real-time and notify technicians of potential issues before they become critical.
- **Robotics and Automation:**
  AI-powered robots are increasingly used in manufacturing to perform repetitive tasks like assembly, packaging, and quality inspection. These robots can work 24/7 without tiring and can be programmed to adapt to different tasks, improving production efficiency and flexibility.

- **Example**: **Tesla's Gigafactories** employ AI-powered robots to assemble electric vehicles. These robots perform tasks like welding and painting with a level of precision that ensures high-quality production.

- **Supply Chain Optimization**:
AI is being used to optimize supply chain management by predicting demand, managing inventories, and analyzing shipping routes. These AI systems ensure that products are delivered on time and in the right quantities, improving efficiency and reducing costs.

  - **Example**: **Amazon's fulfillment centers** use AI to manage inventory and optimize the supply chain. Robots transport products to packing stations, and AI systems predict demand to ensure that the right products are stocked.

5.18 AI in Agriculture and Food Production

AI is also having a profound impact on agriculture, helping farmers improve crop yields, optimize irrigation, and reduce waste. By leveraging AI technologies, agriculture is becoming more sustainable, efficient, and data-driven.

- **Precision Farming**:
AI is enabling precision farming by analyzing data from sensors placed in the field. These sensors monitor variables such as soil moisture, temperature, and nutrient levels. AI then processes this data to provide farmers with insights on how to optimize water usage, fertilization, and pest control.

  - **Example**: **John Deere**, a leading agricultural machinery company, uses AI in their autonomous tractors to optimize planting, harvesting, and fertilization. The AI systems analyze data from sensors to ensure that crops receive the right amount of water and nutrients.

. **AI in Crop Monitoring**:
AI-powered drones and satellites are used to monitor crop health and detect signs of disease or pest infestations. These systems can spot problems early and recommend targeted interventions, reducing the need for widespread pesticide use and minimizing environmental impact.

   ◦ **Example**: **Raptor Maps**, an AI-driven platform, uses drone-captured imagery to assess crop health. Their system helps farmers identify and treat specific areas of their fields that require attention, leading to higher yields and lower costs.

. **AI in Food Processing**:
AI is also used in the food production process, where it helps automate quality control, ensure food safety, and streamline packaging. Computer vision systems can inspect food products for defects, while AI systems monitor and optimize the production line.

   ◦ **Example**: **Zebra Medical Vision**, a healthcare tech company, uses AI to detect signs of contamination in food production lines. Their system helps reduce the risk of foodborne illnesses and ensures that products meet safety standards.

5.19 Conclusion: The Endless Possibilities of AI

As we continue to explore how AI is reshaping our everyday lives, it becomes clear that its potential is virtually limitless. The applications we've discussed are only scratching the surface of what AI can do. From healthcare to agriculture, transportation to retail, AI is revolutionizing industries across the globe.

The future of AI promises even more innovative solutions to long-standing problems, enabling a smarter, more efficient, and more sustainable world. However, as we embrace the potential of AI, it is crucial to remain mindful of the ethical and societal challenges that accompany this rapid advancement.

To ensure that AI benefits everyone, it will require careful planning, regulation, and continued research. But as technology continues to evolve, AI will undoubtedly be at the forefront of shaping the future of human life.

5.20 Key Takeaways

- AI has already started transforming many industries, making processes more efficient, personalized, and innovative.
- The potential for AI to revolutionize sectors like healthcare, manufacturing, agriculture, and transportation is vast and still unfolding.
- While AI offers tremendous benefits, ethical considerations, privacy concerns, and job displacement must be addressed to ensure responsible integration of AI technologies.
- The future of AI looks promising, but continued research, regulation, and collaboration are essential for its responsible development and deployment.

6.1 INTRODUCTION TO AI ETHICS

As AI systems begin to influence critical areas like finance, healthcare, and security, the ethical implications of these technologies become more pronounced. Ethical considerations in AI must address the potential for harm, fairness, and the responsible use of data. AI systems often work behind the scenes, making decisions that affect people's lives, and this can lead to significant challenges. As AI becomes more powerful, society must decide what is acceptable and what is not, creating a framework for responsible use that considers the potential harms and benefits of AI.

Ethics in AI isn't just about preventing harm; it's also about creating systems that serve humanity's best interests and uphold human dignity. This involves tackling issues such as:

- **Bias and fairness** in algorithmic decision-making.
- **Privacy and data protection** when handling personal information.
- **Accountability** for the decisions made by AI systems, especially in high-stakes scenarios.
- **Transparency** regarding how AI systems make decisions, ensuring that people understand why decisions are made.
- **Autonomy** and human oversight, particularly in critical areas like healthcare and criminal justice.

As AI evolves, the moral and ethical landscape will continue to shift, requiring adaptive policies and frameworks to navigate these challenges responsibly. Understanding and addressing these ethical challenges is crucial for a future where AI contributes positively to society.

6.2 Bias and Fairness in AI

6.2.1 The Sources of Bias in AI

AI systems learn from data, and the data used to train them often reflects human biases. These biases can originate from several sources, including:

- **Historical bias**: Many AI systems are trained on historical data that contains discriminatory patterns or practices. For example, historical hiring data may reflect a preference for certain groups over others, leading an AI system to perpetuate those biases in hiring decisions.

- **Sampling bias**: If the data used to train AI models is not representative of the population it is meant to serve, the model will perform poorly on certain groups. For example, an AI model trained on mostly male data might perform less accurately when applied to female patients in medical diagnostics.

- **Label bias**: In supervised learning, the labels (or outcomes) used to train the system might reflect human prejudices. For example, in criminal justice, if a dataset labels people of color as "high-risk" for reoffending based on biased historical data, the AI will learn to replicate those same biases.

6.2.2 Impact of Bias in AI

When AI systems reflect and perpetuate societal biases, the results can be harmful, especially when the system makes critical decisions affecting people's lives. Examples include:

- **Discriminatory hiring practices**: AI systems used by companies to screen resumes or recommend candidates may favor one gender or racial group over others. This can result in qualified candidates being overlooked due to bias inherent in the system.

- **Criminal justice disparities**: AI systems used to assess the likelihood of reoffending may unfairly target minority communities, contributing to racial disparities in the criminal justice system.

- **Healthcare inequality**: AI systems trained on data from predominantly white populations may fail to adequately diagnose or treat individuals from underrepresented groups.

6.2.3 Addressing AI Bias

There are several approaches to reduce bias and promote fairness in AI systems:

- **Diverse datasets**: Ensuring that the data used to train AI systems is representative of diverse populations can help mitigate biases. This includes incorporating demographic diversity and ensuring that underrepresented groups are adequately represented in the data.

- **Fairness metrics**: Researchers are developing fairness metrics that can be applied to AI models to measure and correct bias. These metrics help identify and address disparities in decision outcomes across different groups.

- **Algorithmic audits**: Regular auditing of AI systems by independent bodies or regulatory agencies can help identify and address biases in decision-making. Transparency in model development and performance evaluation can help ensure fairness.

6.3 Privacy and Data Protection

6.3.1 The Importance of Data Privacy

AI systems rely on vast amounts of personal data to function effectively. From medical records and financial transactions to browsing habits and social media activity, this data can reveal sensitive aspects of people's lives. As AI grows in capability, protecting this data becomes more critical.

AI's dependence on data can lead to breaches of privacy in several ways:

- **Data misuse**: Personal data may be collected, stored, or shared without an individual's consent. Without proper oversight, AI companies may exploit data for purposes other than what it was originally intended for.
- **Surveillance**: AI systems, especially in combination with facial recognition technology, have the potential to enable mass surveillance. While surveillance can help with security, it can also infringe on privacy rights, especially when used to track individuals without their knowledge or consent.

6.3.2 Ensuring Privacy in AI

To protect data privacy in AI, several strategies can be employed:

- **Data anonymization**: Anonymizing personal data before using it in AI models ensures that individuals cannot be identified from the data. This helps to mitigate privacy risks while still enabling the AI system to learn valuable insights.
- **Data minimization**: This principle involves collecting only the data necessary for a given purpose and reducing the amount of personal data used in AI models. By minimizing the scope of data, AI systems can reduce the risks associated with data breaches.
- **Robust security measures**: Implementing strong encryption, multi-factor authentication, and other security protocols ensures that personal data remains protected from unauthorized access, hacking, or theft.

6.3.3 Privacy Laws and Regulations

The introduction of regulations like the **General Data Protection Regulation (GDPR)** in the European Union has set a new standard for data privacy and AI. These regulations provide individuals with more control over their personal data and establish clear guidelines for organizations that collect and process data.

- **Right to explanation**: Under GDPR, individuals have the right to know how their data is being used, including any AI algorithms that might be involved in decision-making. This is critical for ensuring transparency and trust in AI systems.

- **Example**: The **California Consumer Privacy Act (CCPA)** also enforces data privacy rights, including the right for individuals to request access to their data, request deletion, and opt out of data collection for purposes like marketing.

6.4.1 The Black Box Problem

As AI systems become increasingly complex, especially in areas like deep learning, understanding how these systems make decisions has become a significant challenge. Many AI models, particularly deep neural networks, operate as "black boxes," meaning their internal processes are opaque and difficult to interpret. This opacity can be problematic, especially when AI systems are used in sensitive or high-stakes domains like healthcare, criminal justice, or hiring.

- **Why is the Black Box Problem an Issue?**
  When a machine learning algorithm makes a decision —such as predicting a patient's risk for a particular disease, or determining whether an applicant is suitable for a job—the decision-making process is often not transparent to humans. This raises several ethical concerns:

  - **Accountability**: If an AI system makes a mistake, it's important to understand why it happened. Without transparency, it can be difficult to assign accountability for errors.

- **Trust**: Users are less likely to trust an AI system if they cannot understand or verify its decision-making process. In fields like healthcare or finance, transparency is critical for building trust.

6.4.2 Explainable AI (XAI)

To address the black box problem, researchers have been working on **Explainable AI (XAI)**, which aims to make AI systems more interpretable and understandable to humans. XAI focuses on creating models that provide clear explanations of their decision-making processes, helping users and stakeholders understand how and why a particular decision was made.

- **Techniques for Explainability**:
  - **Model-agnostic methods**: These approaches can be applied to any AI model and help explain its predictions or decisions. For example, **LIME** (Local Interpretable Model-agnostic Explanations) provides an approximation of a model's decision-making process by generating interpretable surrogate models for complex models.
  - **Feature importance**: This technique ranks the input features based on how much they influence the output decision. For instance, in a medical diagnosis system, it might show which factors (e.g., age, blood pressure, etc.) most influenced the prediction.
  - **Visualization tools**: Some AI models, especially convolutional neural networks (CNNs) used in image processing, can be made more transparent by visualizing what the model "sees" when

making decisions. For example, a tool might highlight areas of an image that contributed most to a diagnosis.

- **Example**: The **IBM Watson Health** system, which has been used in healthcare to analyze medical data, also incorporates explainable AI principles. Watson provides explanations for how it arrives at its diagnoses, enabling doctors to make more informed decisions.

6.4.3 Accountability in AI Decision-Making

One of the core ethical challenges of AI is determining who is responsible when an AI system makes a harmful or erroneous decision. In traditional systems, accountability typically rests with human decision-makers, but with AI systems, accountability can become murky.

- **Liability for AI Errors**:
  If an AI system causes harm—whether by making an incorrect medical diagnosis, recommending a biased hiring decision, or causing an accident in an autonomous vehicle—who should be held accountable? Should the responsibility fall on the developers who created the system, the organization that deployed it, or the AI system itself?
- **Ensuring Accountability**:
  - **Human-in-the-loop systems**: One way to ensure accountability is by keeping humans in the decision-making loop, especially for critical decisions. In areas like healthcare and criminal justice, human oversight can help mitigate the risks of AI errors and prevent harm.
  - **Clear regulatory frameworks**: Governments and regulatory bodies must create clear rules that

outline the responsibilities of AI developers, operators, and users. For example, companies using AI should be required to document and justify how their systems work, including their impact on human decision-making.

6.5 Job Displacement and the Future of Work

6.5.1 The Impact of AI on Employment

One of the most widely discussed implications of AI is its potential to disrupt jobs across many industries. AI's ability to automate tasks that were traditionally performed by humans could lead to job displacement, especially for routine, repetitive jobs that involve low-level cognitive tasks.

- **Which Jobs Are at Risk?**
  AI is most likely to impact jobs that are repetitive and rule-based, such as:
    - **Manufacturing and assembly line work**: AI-powered robots are already being used in factories to perform tasks like assembling products, packaging, and quality control.
    - **Customer service**: AI-powered chatbots and virtual assistants are increasingly being used to handle customer inquiries and support tasks, reducing the need for human customer service representatives.
    - **Data entry and analysis**: AI systems can process and analyze large volumes of data more quickly and accurately than humans, leading to the automation of jobs in data entry, bookkeeping, and basic data analysis.

6.5.2 New Jobs and Opportunities

While AI is expected to eliminate certain jobs, it also has the potential to create new ones. As AI automates tasks, it will create demand for workers with skills in developing, managing, and overseeing AI systems. Some of the emerging job roles include:

- **AI specialists**: As AI technologies evolve, there will be an increased demand for AI engineers, data scientists, machine learning experts, and software developers who can create and maintain AI systems.

- **AI ethicists and auditors**: With increasing concerns around bias, fairness, and transparency, AI ethics specialists will be needed to ensure that AI systems adhere to ethical guidelines. Additionally, AI auditors will play a role in evaluating the fairness and transparency of AI systems.

- **Human-AI collaboration roles**: AI systems will not replace humans entirely; instead, they will complement human workers. Roles that involve collaboration between humans and AI—such as in healthcare, where AI assists doctors with diagnoses—will become more common.

6.5.3 Reskilling and Education for the AI-Driven Future

To mitigate the risks of job displacement, it's essential to focus on reskilling and upskilling the workforce. Preparing workers for an AI-driven economy means equipping them with skills that are less likely to be automated.

- **Key skills for the future**:
  - **AI and machine learning**: Teaching workers how to develop, manage, and work with AI systems will be critical. There are already many online platforms offering AI and data science courses to help people learn these skills.
  - **Creative and interpersonal skills**: While AI can automate routine tasks, creative thinking,

problem-solving, and emotional intelligence will remain valuable. These human-centered skills cannot be easily replicated by AI.

- **Lifelong learning**: The rapid pace of technological change means that workers will need to continually update their skills to stay relevant in the job market. Encouraging a culture of lifelong learning is key to ensuring that workers can adapt to the evolving AI landscape.

6.6 Autonomous Weapons and AI in Warfare

6.6.1 The Rise of Autonomous Weapons

AI technologies are increasingly being incorporated into military applications, raising concerns about the ethical implications of autonomous weapons systems. Autonomous weapons, often referred to as "killer robots," are AI-driven systems capable of identifying and attacking targets without human intervention.

- **Why Autonomous Weapons Are Concerning**:
    - **Lack of accountability**: If an autonomous weapon makes a mistake—such as attacking the wrong target—determining who is responsible can be difficult.
    - **Ethical concerns**: Many argue that it is morally unacceptable to allow machines to make life-and-death decisions, particularly in the context of warfare, where mistakes can result in large-scale casualties.
    - **Escalation of conflict**: The deployment of autonomous weapons may increase the likelihood of conflict, as AI-powered systems could make rapid decisions that escalate tensions without human mediation.

6.6.2 The Call for Regulation

Given the potential dangers of autonomous weapons, there have been increasing calls for international regulations to govern their development and use. Some organizations, including **Human Rights Watch** and the **Campaign to Stop Killer Robots**, have advocated for a global ban on lethal autonomous weapons.

- **Proposals for Regulation**:
  - **Human control**: One approach is to ensure that humans remain in control of the decision to use force, even if AI systems are used for targeting. This would involve designing systems that require human intervention in critical decision-making.
  - **International treaties**: Much like the **Chemical Weapons Convention** or **Nuclear Non-Proliferation Treaty**, countries could come together to create international agreements that ban or strictly regulate autonomous weapons.

6.7 The Future of AI: Opportunities and Challenges

6.7.1 The Transformative Power of AI

Looking toward the future, AI presents enormous opportunities across a wide range of industries. As AI continues to improve, its potential to drive innovation and solve complex global challenges will grow. Some of the most exciting possibilities include:

- **AI in climate change**: AI systems can be used to optimize energy consumption, model climate scenarios, and develop new materials for renewable energy sources.
- **AI in healthcare**: AI-powered diagnostic tools, personalized medicine, and robotic surgeries could revolutionize healthcare by making it more accessible and efficient.

- **AI in education**: AI could provide personalized learning experiences, adapt to individual student needs, and help teachers with administrative tasks, allowing for more focused and effective education.

6.7.2 Challenges to Address

Despite these opportunities, several challenges need to be addressed to ensure that AI is used ethically and responsibly:

- **Ethical concerns**: Bias, fairness, privacy, and accountability must be addressed to prevent AI from causing harm.
- **Regulatory frameworks**: Governments will need to create robust regulations to ensure that AI technologies are used safely and transparently.
- **Public trust**: Building public trust in AI will be essential for its widespread adoption. This requires transparency, accountability, and the responsible development of AI systems.

6.8 Conclusion: Shaping a Responsible AI Future

AI's role in the future is both promising and fraught with challenges. By prioritizing ethics, fairness, privacy, and accountability in the development of AI systems, we can ensure that AI becomes a force for good. As AI continues to evolve, the focus must remain on ensuring that these technologies are developed with human values in mind and are deployed in ways that benefit society as a whole.

CHAPTER 7: AI IN HEALTHCARE

7.1 Introduction to AI in Healthcare

Artificial intelligence has the potential to transform healthcare by improving diagnosis, treatment, and patient care. AI technologies, particularly in machine learning and deep learning, can analyze vast amounts of medical data to assist doctors in making faster, more accurate decisions. In areas such as medical imaging, drug discovery, personalized medicine, and patient management, AI is already making significant strides.

The healthcare industry is increasingly adopting AI for various applications, from routine tasks to more complex decision-making processes. By leveraging AI, healthcare providers can improve efficiency, reduce costs, and enhance patient outcomes. However, this also raises ethical questions, including concerns about data privacy, the potential for bias, and the role of human oversight in AI-driven decisions.

7.2 AI in Medical Imaging

One of the most prominent applications of AI in healthcare is in the field of medical imaging. AI-powered systems, particularly those based on deep learning algorithms, can help analyze medical images like X-rays, CT scans, MRIs, and ultrasounds. These systems are able to detect abnormalities such as tumors, fractures, and other medical conditions faster and often more accurately than human radiologists.

- **Deep Learning for Image Recognition**: AI models trained on large datasets of medical images can learn to identify patterns that may be difficult for human doctors to detect. For example, deep learning algorithms are used to detect early signs of cancer in mammograms or analyze retinal scans to identify diabetic retinopathy.

- **Improved Diagnosis**: AI can assist doctors by highlighting areas of concern in images and suggesting possible diagnoses. This can reduce the chances of missed diagnoses and help doctors prioritize the most urgent cases.

- **Efficiency Gains**: AI can automate the initial stages of medical imaging analysis, allowing radiologists to focus on more complex cases, which can increase overall productivity and reduce waiting times for patients.

7.3 AI in Drug Discovery

AI has the potential to revolutionize drug discovery, an area that traditionally involves lengthy and expensive processes. By using AI to analyze biological data, researchers can identify potential drug candidates more quickly and accurately.

- **Predictive Modeling**: AI models can predict how molecules will behave in the body and identify which compounds are likely to have therapeutic effects. This allows pharmaceutical companies to focus their research on the most promising compounds, reducing the time and cost of bringing a drug to market.

- **AI and Genomics**: AI can also be used to analyze genomic data and uncover new insights into the genetic factors that contribute to diseases. By identifying genetic markers and pathways associated with various conditions, AI can help develop personalized treatments that are tailored to an individual's genetic makeup.

- **Speeding Up the Process**: With AI, pharmaceutical companies can simulate how drugs interact with the body, predict side effects, and identify potential risks before clinical trials begin. This can shorten the drug development timeline and lead to more targeted, effective treatments.

7.4 AI in Personalized Medicine

Personalized medicine refers to the practice of tailoring medical treatment to the individual characteristics of each patient. AI plays a crucial role in enabling personalized medicine by analyzing vast amounts of data, such as genetic profiles, medical histories, and lifestyle information, to recommend the most effective treatments.

- **Genomic Data and AI**: AI can help decode complex genomic data, identifying specific genetic mutations that may impact a patient's response to treatment. For example, AI systems can assist oncologists in choosing the best cancer treatment based on the patient's unique genetic profile.

- **Predictive Analytics**: By analyzing a patient's medical records, AI can predict the likelihood of developing certain conditions, such as heart disease or diabetes, and recommend preventive measures or treatments. This allows for earlier interventions and better outcomes.

- **Tailored Treatment Plans**: AI can also assist in developing individualized treatment plans by considering the patient's age, gender, lifestyle, and other factors that influence health outcomes. This ensures that patients receive the most appropriate care based on their unique needs.

7.5 AI in Clinical Decision Support

AI can assist healthcare providers in making clinical decisions by providing evidence-based recommendations and identifying patterns in patient data. Clinical decision support systems (CDSS) use AI algorithms to analyze patient information and generate recommendations for diagnosis, treatment, and care management.

- **Predictive Models**: AI can predict patient outcomes based on historical data, helping doctors assess the likelihood of recovery, complications, or readmission. For example, AI can predict which patients are at high risk for sepsis and recommend early interventions.

- **Real-Time Decision Making**: AI systems can provide real-time decision support during patient consultations, allowing doctors to make informed decisions more quickly. This can be especially valuable in emergency care settings where rapid decision-making is critical.

- **Reducing Medical Errors**: By providing doctors with data-driven recommendations and flagging potential errors or inconsistencies in patient records, AI can help reduce medical errors and improve patient safety.

7.6 AI in Patient Monitoring and Management

AI can also enhance patient monitoring and management, particularly for patients with chronic conditions. By using AI-powered sensors, wearables, and remote monitoring tools, healthcare providers can track patient health in real-time and intervene when necessary.

- **Wearables and IoT Devices**: Wearable devices, such as smartwatches and fitness trackers, can monitor vital signs like heart rate, blood pressure, and oxygen levels. AI can analyze this data in real-time, detecting early warning signs of health issues and alerting healthcare providers to take action.

- **Remote Patient Monitoring**: AI can enable healthcare providers to remotely monitor patients, reducing the need for frequent in-person visits. This is especially beneficial for patients with chronic conditions like diabetes or hypertension, who need regular monitoring and care.

- **Personalized Alerts**: AI systems can analyze patient data and generate personalized alerts for both patients and healthcare providers. For example, if a patient's blood sugar levels rise above a certain threshold, the system can send an alert to both the patient and their doctor, prompting timely intervention.

7.7 AI in Surgery

AI's impact on surgery is profound, providing tools that assist surgeons in planning and performing operations with greater precision. Robotic surgery, guided by AI, is revolutionizing the field, offering minimally invasive options that can reduce recovery times and improve outcomes.

- **Robotic-Assisted Surgery**: Robotic systems, such as the **da Vinci Surgical System**, enable surgeons to perform operations with a high degree of precision. AI algorithms guide the robot's movements, ensuring that the surgical tools remain steady and accurate. This is particularly useful in delicate surgeries, such as prostate or heart surgery, where precision is critical.

- **AI in Preoperative Planning**: Before surgery, AI can assist in planning the procedure by analyzing medical images and predicting potential complications. For example, AI can assess the location and size of tumors in cancer patients and help design a surgical approach that minimizes risks.

- **Postoperative Care**: After surgery, AI can help monitor patients for signs of complications, such as infection or blood clots. AI-driven systems can continuously analyze patient data from sensors and alert medical staff to potential issues before they become critical.

7.8 AI in Healthcare Administration

AI is not only transforming patient care but also streamlining healthcare administration. Administrative tasks, which traditionally consume a significant amount of time and resources, can be automated using AI technologies, improving efficiency and reducing costs.

- **Automated Medical Coding**: AI systems can automatically assign medical codes to diagnoses, treatments, and procedures based on patient records. This reduces human error, speeds up the billing process, and ensures that healthcare providers are reimbursed properly.

- **Natural Language Processing (NLP)**: NLP technologies enable AI to process and understand unstructured data, such as notes from doctors, patient histories, and research papers. This can automate tasks like summarizing patient records, identifying relevant research findings, and assisting in medical documentation.

- **Scheduling and Resource Allocation**: AI can optimize scheduling and resource allocation in healthcare facilities, ensuring that staff, equipment, and rooms are used efficiently. For example, AI systems can predict patient demand and suggest the best allocation of resources, reducing waiting times and improving overall hospital performance.

7.9 Ethical Considerations in AI Healthcare

While the potential benefits of AI in healthcare are immense, there are several ethical challenges that must be addressed to ensure that AI systems are used responsibly and safely.

- **Data Privacy**: Healthcare data is highly sensitive, and AI systems require access to vast amounts of patient information to function effectively. Ensuring that this data is kept secure and used ethically is a major concern. AI systems must adhere to strict privacy regulations, such as the **Health Insurance Portability and Accountability Act (HIPAA)** in the U.S., to prevent misuse and breaches.

- **Bias and Fairness**: AI models can inherit biases present in the data they are trained on, leading to biased outcomes in healthcare. For example, if a model is trained on data that predominantly represents one demographic, it may not perform as well for other groups. Ensuring that AI systems are fair and unbiased is essential to avoid discrimination in healthcare decisions.

- **Informed Consent**: As AI becomes more involved in patient care, it is important for patients to be informed about the role of AI in their treatment. Informed consent must include a clear explanation of how AI will be used in their diagnosis and treatment, ensuring that patients are comfortable with AI-driven decisions.

- **Human Oversight**: While AI can enhance decision-making, it is crucial to maintain human oversight, especially in life-threatening situations. AI should assist healthcare professionals, not replace them. Ensuring that healthcare workers can interpret AI recommendations and make the final decisions is important to preserve the human element in patient care.

7.10 AI's Role in Pandemic Response and Public Health

The COVID-19 pandemic highlighted the critical role that AI can play in healthcare, from predicting outbreaks to developing treatments and vaccines. AI is also being used in public health efforts to track disease spread, analyze trends, and inform policy decisions.

- **Predicting Disease Spread**: AI models can analyze data from various sources, such as social media, travel patterns, and hospital reports, to predict the spread of infectious diseases. For instance, AI-powered platforms were used during the COVID-19 pandemic to predict the number of cases, identify hotspots, and forecast the need for medical supplies.

. **Vaccine Development**: AI has accelerated the process of vaccine development by analyzing protein structures, predicting vaccine candidates, and optimizing the design of clinical trials. AI tools were instrumental in identifying potential vaccine candidates for COVID-19, significantly shortening the timeline for development.

. **Remote Diagnostics and Telemedicine**: The pandemic underscored the importance of telemedicine and remote healthcare services. AI is being used to enhance telemedicine platforms, providing tools for remote diagnosis, monitoring, and treatment. AI-powered chatbots, for example, can conduct preliminary screenings and offer advice before patients speak to a doctor.

7.11 Challenges and Barriers to AI Adoption in Healthcare

Despite its potential, AI adoption in healthcare faces several challenges that need to be overcome.

. **Integration with Legacy Systems**: Many healthcare systems still rely on outdated technology, making it difficult to integrate AI solutions. Hospitals and clinics must modernize their infrastructure to support AI-driven tools, which can be costly and time-consuming.

. **Regulatory Approvals**: AI-based healthcare tools must undergo rigorous testing and approval processes before they can be widely adopted. Regulatory bodies like the **FDA (Food and Drug Administration)** in the U.S. and the **European Medicines Agency (EMA)** require that AI systems meet high standards of safety and efficacy before they are deployed in clinical settings.

- **Resistance to Change**: Healthcare professionals may be reluctant to adopt AI technologies, especially if they feel that these systems threaten their expertise or job security. Providing training and emphasizing the benefits of AI in supporting healthcare workers can help overcome this resistance.

- **Cost of Implementation**: The cost of developing, implementing, and maintaining AI technologies can be prohibitive for many healthcare institutions, particularly in resource-limited settings. Governments and organizations need to consider ways to make AI more accessible and affordable, especially for underserved communities.

7.12 Future Directions in AI Healthcare

Looking ahead, the integration of AI in healthcare is expected to continue growing, with advancements in areas like **personalized medicine**, **predictive analytics**, and **robotic surgery**. As AI evolves, its role in healthcare will expand to include:

- **AI in Mental Health**: AI tools could assist in diagnosing and treating mental health conditions by analyzing patient data, such as speech patterns, social media activity, and behavioral trends.

- **AI for Aging Populations**: AI can play a significant role in managing the healthcare needs of aging populations, assisting in areas such as fall detection, chronic disease management, and cognitive decline monitoring.

- **Collaborative AI Systems**: The future of healthcare may see more collaborative AI systems, where AI works alongside healthcare providers to co-create solutions tailored to individual patients. This partnership will help streamline workflows and improve overall care.

7.13 Conclusion

AI has the potential to revolutionize healthcare by improving efficiency, accuracy, and accessibility. From medical imaging to drug discovery and personalized treatment, AI is already making a significant impact. However, ethical considerations, data privacy, and regulatory challenges must be addressed to ensure that AI is used responsibly and effectively in healthcare. As technology continues to advance, AI will likely play an increasingly prominent role in shaping the future of healthcare, offering new opportunities for better patient outcomes and more efficient healthcare systems.

CHAPTER 8: AI IN BUSINESS AND INDUSTRY

8.1 Introduction to AI in Business

AI has revolutionized the way businesses operate across industries, from improving customer experience to optimizing internal processes. By leveraging machine learning, natural language processing, and predictive analytics, businesses can gain insights from large datasets, streamline operations, and drive innovation. AI's integration into business strategies has created competitive advantages, enhanced decision-making, and opened new revenue streams.

In this chapter, we will explore how AI is reshaping key sectors such as finance, retail, supply chain management, and human resources, as well as the ethical implications of AI adoption in business settings.

8.2 AI in Finance

AI is transforming the finance industry by enabling faster, more accurate decision-making and automating many manual processes. Financial institutions are increasingly adopting AI technologies to improve customer service, mitigate risks, and drive efficiencies.

- **Algorithmic Trading**: AI-driven algorithms are used to analyze market data and execute trades at high speeds. These algorithms can identify patterns, predict market trends, and make buy or sell decisions without human intervention. High-frequency trading, powered by AI, has become a crucial part of modern financial markets.

- **Fraud Detection**: AI is being used to detect fraudulent activity by analyzing transaction data in real-time. Machine learning algorithms can recognize unusual patterns in spending, flagging suspicious transactions before they are processed. This reduces financial fraud and minimizes the damage caused by cybercriminals.

- **Credit Scoring and Risk Management**: AI can improve credit scoring models by analyzing a wider range of data beyond traditional credit reports. Machine learning algorithms can evaluate a person's creditworthiness by examining transaction history, spending habits, and even social media activity. This provides a more accurate and comprehensive risk assessment, leading to better-informed lending decisions.

- **Customer Service and Chatbots**: AI-powered chatbots and virtual assistants are increasingly used in the finance sector to handle customer inquiries, process transactions, and provide personalized financial advice. These systems can interact with customers in real-time, offering tailored solutions and improving overall customer satisfaction.

8.3 AI in Retail

In the retail sector, AI is transforming how businesses interact with customers, manage inventory, and optimize supply chains. By using AI to analyze consumer behavior and personalize shopping experiences, retailers can increase sales, improve customer satisfaction, and reduce costs.

- **Personalized Recommendations**: AI algorithms analyze customer data, such as browsing history, purchase patterns, and preferences, to provide personalized product recommendations. This not only enhances the customer shopping experience but also increases conversion rates and sales.

- **Inventory Management**: AI-powered systems help retailers manage inventory by predicting demand, tracking stock levels, and optimizing supply chain logistics. These systems can forecast product demand, reducing overstocking or understocking issues and ensuring products are available when customers need them.

- **Customer Sentiment Analysis**: Retailers use AI to analyze customer feedback from various channels, such as social media, reviews, and surveys. Sentiment analysis helps businesses understand how customers feel about products, services, or brands, enabling them to make informed decisions on product development, marketing strategies, and customer service improvements.

- **Virtual Try-Ons**: AI-powered augmented reality (AR) tools allow customers to virtually try on clothes, accessories, or makeup products before making a purchase. This enhances the shopping experience by providing a more interactive and personalized way to explore products.

8.4 AI in Manufacturing and Supply Chain

AI is playing a significant role in optimizing manufacturing processes and supply chain management. By using AI for predictive maintenance, demand forecasting, and production optimization, companies can reduce costs, improve efficiency, and enhance product quality.

- **Predictive Maintenance**: AI can predict when machines and equipment are likely to fail by analyzing sensor data and historical performance. Predictive maintenance reduces downtime by allowing companies to perform maintenance before equipment breaks down, improving overall production efficiency.

- **Demand Forecasting**: AI algorithms analyze historical data, market trends, and external factors to forecast demand for products. By accurately predicting future demand, manufacturers can adjust production schedules, optimize inventory levels, and reduce waste.

- **Robotic Process Automation (RPA)**: AI-driven robots are increasingly being used in manufacturing facilities for tasks such as assembly, packaging, and quality control. These robots can work around the clock without fatigue, improving production rates and reducing labor costs.

- **Supply Chain Optimization**: AI can optimize supply chains by analyzing data from various sources, including suppliers, logistics providers, and customers. AI algorithms can help identify the most efficient routes, predict potential disruptions, and recommend adjustments to reduce costs and improve delivery times.

8.5 AI in Human Resources

AI is transforming human resources (HR) by automating administrative tasks, improving recruitment processes, and enhancing employee management. With the help of AI, HR departments can streamline operations and make data-driven decisions about talent acquisition and employee performance.

- **Recruitment and Hiring**: AI-powered recruitment tools can analyze resumes, cover letters, and online profiles to identify the best candidates for a job. These systems can also conduct initial screenings, schedule interviews, and assess applicants' suitability for roles based on their skills and experience. This reduces the time spent on manual recruitment tasks and ensures that HR departments can focus on high-value activities.

- **Employee Engagement and Retention**: AI can help improve employee engagement by analyzing feedback, performance metrics, and social interactions. By identifying patterns in employee satisfaction and performance, AI tools can recommend strategies to boost morale and reduce turnover.

- **Training and Development**: AI-powered learning platforms can personalize training programs for employees, tailoring the content to their specific needs and learning styles. These platforms can also track employees' progress and provide feedback, ensuring that training programs are effective and aligned with company goals.

- **Workforce Analytics**: AI can analyze workforce data to uncover trends and insights about employee performance, productivity, and organizational health. HR departments can use this data to make informed decisions about staffing, promotions, and compensation.

8.6 Ethical Implications of AI in Business

As AI becomes increasingly integrated into business operations, several ethical concerns must be addressed to ensure responsible usage.

- **Bias and Fairness**: AI systems can inherit biases from the data they are trained on, leading to unfair outcomes in areas such as hiring, lending, or customer service. For instance, if an AI hiring tool is trained on data that favors a particular demographic, it may unintentionally discriminate against other groups. Businesses must ensure that AI models are designed to be fair and unbiased by using diverse datasets and regularly auditing their systems for discriminatory outcomes.

- **Job Displacement**: Automation powered by AI has the potential to displace jobs, especially in sectors like manufacturing and customer service. While AI can improve efficiency, businesses must consider the social implications of workforce displacement and explore strategies for retraining and upskilling workers.

- **Transparency and Accountability**: Businesses must be transparent about how they use AI and ensure accountability in decision-making. Customers, employees, and stakeholders need to understand how AI systems work, especially when AI is involved in critical decisions such as hiring, promotions, or lending.

- **Data Privacy**: As businesses collect more data to feed AI systems, protecting customer and employee privacy becomes a major concern. Companies must implement strong data protection measures to safeguard sensitive information and comply with data privacy regulations like GDPR.

8.7 Future Directions of AI in Business

As AI continues to evolve, businesses will find new ways to leverage its capabilities to gain competitive advantages and create innovative solutions. Some potential future directions include:

- **AI-Powered Customer Experiences**: Future AI systems will be even more capable of providing personalized, real-time interactions with customers, anticipating their needs and offering tailored solutions. AI will become more adept at understanding and responding to customer emotions, creating more human-like interactions.

- **AI in Marketing**: AI will play an increasingly significant role in marketing, helping businesses create hyper-targeted campaigns based on individual customer preferences and behaviors. Predictive analytics will enable businesses to anticipate customer needs and offer personalized promotions or recommendations.

- **Collaborative AI**: The future of AI in business may involve more collaboration between AI systems and human employees. AI tools will serve as decision support systems, providing data-driven insights and recommendations that humans can use to make more informed decisions.

- **AI for Sustainability**: AI can help businesses optimize their operations for sustainability by reducing energy consumption, minimizing waste, and optimizing supply chains. AI-driven sustainability initiatives will become increasingly important as companies strive to meet environmental goals and comply with regulatory standards.

8.8 Conclusion

AI is transforming the landscape of business and industry, driving efficiency, innovation, and growth across various sectors. From finance to manufacturing, retail, and human resources, AI is helping businesses optimize their operations, improve customer experiences, and make better decisions. However, the ethical challenges of AI adoption—such as bias, job displacement, and data privacy—must be carefully managed to ensure that AI is used responsibly. Looking ahead, businesses that embrace AI will be better positioned to adapt to an increasingly competitive and dynamic marketplace.

CHAPTER 9: AI IN TRANSPORTATION

9.1 Introduction to AI in Transportation

The transportation industry is one of the most dynamic sectors, constantly evolving to meet growing demand for efficiency, safety, and sustainability. AI is playing a transformative role in reshaping how goods and people move, from autonomous vehicles to smart traffic systems and predictive maintenance. With the integration of machine learning, computer vision, and data analytics, AI is helping to optimize transportation networks, improve safety, and create more sustainable solutions.

In this chapter, we will explore the different ways AI is being utilized in transportation, including self-driving cars, traffic management, logistics, and air travel.

9.2 Autonomous Vehicles (Self-Driving Cars)

Autonomous vehicles (AVs) are perhaps the most well-known application of AI in transportation. These vehicles use AI-powered systems to navigate, control, and drive themselves, with minimal or no human intervention.

- **How Autonomous Vehicles Work**: Self-driving cars rely on a combination of sensors (such as LiDAR, radar, and cameras), machine learning algorithms, and complex decision-making systems to perceive their environment, make real-time decisions, and navigate roads safely. AI is responsible for processing data from these sensors, detecting obstacles, understanding traffic patterns, and making driving decisions in real time.

- **Safety and Efficiency**: Autonomous vehicles have the potential to drastically reduce accidents caused by human error, such as distracted driving or impaired driving. By using AI to continuously analyze data, AVs can respond to dangerous situations faster than human drivers, reducing collisions and improving road safety. Additionally, AI can optimize driving patterns to enhance fuel efficiency and reduce emissions.

- **Challenges to Adoption**: While autonomous vehicles offer significant benefits, there are several challenges to overcome before they can be fully integrated into society. These include regulatory hurdles, public acceptance, technological reliability, and the need for robust infrastructure. Moreover, ethical dilemmas, such as decision-making in accident scenarios, must be addressed to ensure that AI systems make the right choices in critical situations.

9.3 AI in Traffic Management

AI is revolutionizing how traffic is managed, especially in urban environments where congestion, pollution, and inefficiency are common problems. Smart traffic management systems use AI to optimize traffic flow, reduce congestion, and improve overall urban mobility.

- **Smart Traffic Lights**: AI-powered traffic lights use real-time data to adjust signal timings dynamically. By analyzing traffic patterns, weather conditions, and pedestrian movement, these systems can optimize traffic flow, reducing wait times at intersections and minimizing congestion. Some cities are already using AI-driven systems to reduce traffic jams and improve commuter experience.

- **Predictive Traffic Analytics**: AI can predict traffic patterns and road conditions by analyzing data from sensors, cameras, and GPS devices. This predictive capability allows cities to implement preemptive measures, such as rerouting traffic or deploying traffic officers in areas with expected congestion. It can also assist drivers by providing real-time information on the best routes to take.

- **Autonomous Fleet Management**: AI is used in fleet management systems to optimize routes, improve fuel efficiency, and manage maintenance schedules for commercial fleets. By analyzing traffic data and vehicle performance, AI can predict when a vehicle needs maintenance or when it should be rerouted to avoid delays.

9.4 AI in Logistics and Supply Chain Management

AI is streamlining logistics and supply chain operations, which are critical to the global economy. From warehousing to route optimization, AI technologies are enabling businesses to operate more efficiently, reduce costs, and improve service delivery.

- **Route Optimization**: AI can analyze factors such as traffic, weather, and road conditions to determine the most efficient route for transportation. Logistics companies can use AI to reduce delivery times, cut fuel costs, and enhance customer satisfaction by providing real-time tracking information.

- **Predictive Maintenance**: Similar to its application in manufacturing, AI can be used in logistics to predict when delivery vehicles will need maintenance. This helps prevent breakdowns and delays, ensuring that shipments are delivered on time.

- **Autonomous Drones and Delivery**: AI-powered drones are being developed for last-mile delivery, offering a faster and more efficient alternative to traditional delivery methods. By using computer vision and machine learning, drones can navigate urban environments, deliver packages to precise locations, and avoid obstacles. This innovation could revolutionize e-commerce and package delivery industries, particularly in remote or densely populated areas.

- **Warehouse Automation**: AI is used to automate warehouses through robotic systems that can pick, sort, and transport goods without human intervention. These systems use machine learning to improve accuracy and efficiency over time, reducing the need for manual labor and improving operational speed.

9.5 AI in Air Transportation

AI's influence on air transportation is increasingly visible, with applications spanning from flight scheduling and maintenance to in-flight operations and autonomous aircraft.

- **Flight Scheduling and Optimization**: Airlines use AI to optimize flight schedules and ensure that planes are operating at maximum efficiency. AI can analyze a wide range of factors, including weather patterns, air traffic, and aircraft performance, to minimize delays and improve on-time performance.

- **Predictive Maintenance**: Predictive analytics is used in aviation to monitor the health of aircraft engines, avionics, and other critical systems. AI-driven systems analyze data from sensors embedded in the aircraft to predict potential failures before they occur, reducing downtime and enhancing safety.

- **Autonomous Aircraft**: While fully autonomous commercial flights are not yet a reality, AI is being integrated into unmanned aerial vehicles (UAVs) for tasks such as cargo delivery, surveillance, and monitoring. Researchers are exploring the possibility of autonomous passenger aircraft, which could eventually reshape the air travel industry by reducing human error and lowering operational costs.

9.6 AI in Maritime Transportation

AI is also making strides in maritime transportation, where it is being used to enhance navigation, improve safety, and optimize operations.

- **Autonomous Ships**: AI is being used to develop autonomous ships that can navigate oceans and seas with minimal human intervention. These vessels rely on AI-powered systems to monitor their surroundings, detect obstacles, and make real-time decisions about navigation.

- **Fleet Management and Route Optimization**: Similar to the logistics sector, AI is used to optimize shipping routes for maritime fleets. By analyzing data such as ocean currents, weather patterns, and cargo loads, AI can help reduce fuel consumption and increase shipping efficiency.

- **Port Automation**: AI is being employed in ports to automate processes such as container handling, vessel docking, and cargo unloading. AI-powered robots and drones are improving efficiency, reducing turnaround times, and lowering costs in the shipping industry.

9.7 Ethical Considerations in AI in Transportation

The use of AI in transportation raises important ethical questions, particularly regarding safety, privacy, and accountability.

- **Safety and Liability**: In the event of an accident involving an autonomous vehicle, questions about liability and accountability arise. If an AI system makes a decision that leads to a crash, it may be unclear whether the responsibility lies with the manufacturer, the software developer, or the owner of the vehicle.

- **Privacy and Data Security**: Autonomous vehicles and

AI-driven traffic systems collect vast amounts of data, including location, behavior, and driving patterns. Ensuring that this data is securely stored and used responsibly is critical to maintaining public trust in AI technologies.

. **Job Displacement**: As AI continues to automate various aspects of transportation, there is concern about the displacement of jobs, particularly for truck drivers, taxi drivers, and pilots. The transportation sector must address these concerns by providing retraining opportunities and ensuring a smooth transition to new roles for affected workers.

9.8 Future Directions in AI for Transportation

The future of AI in transportation holds great promise, with advancements likely to create safer, more efficient, and sustainable transportation networks.

. **Integrated Mobility Systems**: Future transportation networks will likely be fully integrated, where AI manages not only individual vehicles but also public transportation, bicycles, ride-sharing services, and more. This integrated system will optimize travel for individuals and reduce congestion in cities.

. **Sustainability and Green Technologies**: AI will play a key role in the development of sustainable transportation solutions. Electric autonomous vehicles, smart traffic systems, and AI-driven logistics solutions will help reduce carbon emissions and promote greener transportation alternatives.

. **AI in Space Transportation**: Looking further into the future, AI could also play a crucial role in space transportation, helping to navigate spacecraft, manage interplanetary travel, and optimize resource allocation for long-term space missions.

9.9 Conclusion

AI is revolutionizing the transportation industry by improving safety, efficiency, and sustainability. From autonomous vehicles to smart traffic systems and logistics optimization, AI is reshaping how we move goods and people across the globe. While challenges remain in terms of ethics, regulation, and public acceptance, the continued development of AI technologies promises a future where transportation is safer, more efficient, and environmentally friendly.

CHAPTER 10: THE FUTURE OF AI

10.1 Introduction to the Future of AI

The future of artificial intelligence is an exciting and rapidly evolving frontier. As we look toward the next decade and beyond, AI is poised to transform virtually every aspect of our lives—affecting how we work, communicate, create, and interact with the world. With advancements in machine learning, quantum computing, and neural networks, the potential for AI to revolutionize industries, solve global challenges, and create new opportunities is limitless.

However, with great potential comes great responsibility. As AI continues to advance, we must grapple with questions about its ethical use, potential risks, and the social implications of widespread AI adoption. This chapter explores the future trends, potential breakthroughs, and challenges that AI is likely to face in the coming years.

10.2 Advancements in AI Research

AI research is progressing at an unprecedented rate, with breakthroughs occurring regularly in areas such as natural language processing, reinforcement learning, and neural networks. These advancements are driving improvements in the capabilities of AI systems, allowing them to perform more complex tasks and make decisions with greater accuracy.

- **Deep Learning and Neural Networks**: The development of more sophisticated deep learning algorithms will enable AI systems to better understand context, process vast amounts of data, and make more informed decisions. Future neural networks will likely mimic the human brain even more closely, enabling AI to perform tasks that require intuition, creativity, and abstract reasoning.

- **Quantum Computing and AI**: Quantum computing, which harnesses the principles of quantum mechanics, holds the potential to exponentially increase computational power. By leveraging quantum computing, AI systems could solve complex problems that are currently beyond the reach of classical computers. This could lead to breakthroughs in areas like drug discovery, climate modeling, and optimization problems.

- **General Artificial Intelligence (AGI)**: One of the most ambitious goals in AI research is the development of Artificial General Intelligence (AGI)—a machine capable of performing any cognitive task that a human can do. While current AI systems are designed to excel in narrow, specialized tasks (known as narrow AI), AGI would possess the ability to learn, adapt, and perform a wide range of tasks across multiple domains. Although AGI remains a distant goal, progress in machine learning and neural networks brings us one step closer to its realization.

10.3 AI in Healthcare: The Next Frontier

AI has already made significant strides in healthcare, but the future promises even more profound innovations. AI's ability to analyze complex medical data and assist in diagnosis is poised to transform healthcare delivery, making it more personalized, efficient, and accessible.

- **Precision Medicine**: AI will help advance precision medicine by enabling doctors to tailor treatments based on individual genetic profiles and health histories. AI algorithms can analyze vast amounts of genetic data to predict how different patients will respond to specific treatments, reducing trial-and-error approaches and improving patient outcomes.

- **AI in Drug Discovery**: The process of developing new

drugs is time-consuming and costly. AI can speed up this process by analyzing vast datasets of chemical compounds, biological data, and patient information to identify promising drug candidates. AI-driven drug discovery platforms could help accelerate the development of treatments for diseases such as cancer, Alzheimer's, and rare genetic disorders.

- **Robotic Surgery and Virtual Health Assistants**: AI-powered robots are already assisting in surgery, with the potential to improve precision and reduce recovery times. In the future, virtual health assistants—powered by AI—could provide patients with 24/7 access to medical advice, schedule appointments, and monitor their health, offering a more personalized approach to healthcare.

10.4 AI in the Workplace and the Future of Jobs

As AI continues to integrate into business and industry, its impact on the workforce will be significant. Automation powered by AI has already begun to replace certain manual and repetitive jobs, but the future will likely see the emergence of new roles that require human-AI collaboration.

- **AI-Augmented Work**: Rather than fully replacing human workers, AI will augment human capabilities, allowing employees to perform tasks more efficiently and effectively. In fields like healthcare, finance, and education, AI can assist with data analysis, decision-making, and customer service, empowering workers to focus on more complex and creative tasks.

- **Job Displacement and Retraining**: While AI will create new job opportunities, it will also lead to the displacement of workers in industries that are highly susceptible to automation, such as manufacturing, transportation, and customer service. To mitigate the effects of job displacement, governments and businesses will need to invest in retraining and reskilling programs to help workers transition to new roles.

- **Human-AI Collaboration**: The future of work will be characterized by collaboration between humans and AI systems. AI will serve as a tool to enhance human capabilities, rather than replace them entirely. In creative fields such as design, art, and content creation, AI can assist with brainstorming, content generation, and idea refinement, while humans provide the creativity and emotional intelligence that AI lacks.

10.5 AI in Society: Ethical and Social Implications

As AI becomes more integrated into daily life, society will need to address important ethical and social considerations. The future of AI will require careful thought and regulation to ensure that it is used for the benefit of all people, without exacerbating inequalities or creating new risks.

- **Bias and Fairness**: AI systems are only as good as the data they are trained on. If these datasets reflect biases present in society, AI systems may perpetuate or even amplify these biases, leading to unfair outcomes. To ensure fairness, AI systems must be trained on diverse, representative datasets, and organizations must regularly audit AI systems to detect and correct biases.

- **Privacy and Surveillance**: As AI systems collect and analyze vast amounts of personal data, privacy concerns will become increasingly important. Governments and companies will need to establish clear policies and regulations to protect individuals' privacy while balancing the benefits of AI-driven insights and services.

- **AI Governance and Accountability**: As AI systems become more autonomous and capable of making critical decisions, it will be essential to establish frameworks for AI governance. Who is responsible when an AI system makes a harmful decision? How can we ensure transparency and accountability in AI-driven processes? These questions will need to be addressed to ensure that AI is used ethically and responsibly.

- **Global Impact and Inequality**: The benefits of AI are not equally distributed. While developed countries and large corporations may reap the rewards of AI advancements, there is a risk that AI could exacerbate global inequalities, leaving disadvantaged populations behind. Ensuring that AI benefits all of humanity will require international cooperation and investment in AI development for the public good.

10.6 The Road Ahead: AI in Space Exploration and Beyond

AI's potential extends beyond Earth, with applications in space exploration, environmental monitoring, and even the search for extraterrestrial life. As AI systems become more advanced, they will play an increasingly important role in shaping humanity's future in space.

- **AI in Space Exploration**: AI is already being used in space missions to assist with navigation, data analysis, and autonomous decision-making. AI-powered systems help spacecraft navigate to distant planets, monitor spacecraft health, and analyze scientific data. In the future, AI could assist with autonomous exploration of Mars and other planets, analyzing samples and making real-time decisions in environments where human intervention is limited.

- **Environmental Monitoring and Climate Change**: AI can help address the pressing global issue of climate change by analyzing environmental data and predicting future trends. AI-powered models can predict weather patterns, monitor deforestation, and optimize energy usage, helping governments and organizations take action to mitigate the effects of climate change.

10.7 Conclusion: Embracing the Future of AI

The future of AI holds immense promise, offering solutions to some of the world's most pressing challenges while also raising new questions about ethics, governance, and social impact. As AI continues to evolve, it will play an increasingly integral role in shaping industries, economies, and societies. To harness its full potential, we must embrace its capabilities responsibly, ensuring that AI benefits all people, promotes fairness, and aligns with our values.

The journey of AI is just beginning, and as we continue to innovate and push the boundaries of what's possible, the future of AI will undoubtedly be an exciting, transformative force in our world.

www.ingramcontent.com/pod-product-compliance
Lightning Source LLC
LaVergne TN
LVHW092340060326
832902LV00008B/736